"Melissa shares how to be content and happy in our home, inspiring our home with the things we love and the people we cherish."

Ann Voskamp, *New York Times* bestselling author of *One Thousand Gifts*

"Melissa Michaels' book *The Inspired Room* is full of smart, practical advice and packed with inspiration to spare. The photos are gorgeous and accompanied by helpful tips and details, and the writing lifts you up and makes you excited to dive into home decor headfirst!"

Sherry Petersik, *New York Times* bestselling author of *Young House Love*

"I just love Melissa's approach to decorating to give yourself time to let the process of decorating happen in your home, give yourself grace, and enjoy the process. She really speaks to my heart and brings out the best in me when it comes to my home."

Rachel Dowd, *Sweet and Simple Home* (blog)

"I've read *The Inspired Room* cover to cover, and it's going to be one of the most useful books I've ever owned. Melissa is a great teacher, and designer, and is so very humble, and she just has that 'you can do it' spirit about her."

Sandy Coughlin, *Reluctant Entertainer* (blog)

"*Love the Home You Have* is what all overwhelmed moms need—confirmation that they can find joy in the small things no matter the size of their home or the amount of stuff they have (or do not have)."

Susan Heid, *The Confident Mom* (blog)

"*Love the Home You Have* speaks not only to the well-organized mom who wants to create a beautiful and lovely home, but to the disorganized, stressed, often-overwhelmed mom (me) who just needs some reassurance about what a home truly is. Melissa has a passion for life and beauty that translates into one of the best (and most needed) books I have read in a long time. Well done!"

Amanda Rettke, *I Am Baker* (blog)

"Melissa feels it's important to 'use what quality pieces you have to become the building blocks for your style.' There are so many welcome tips in *The Inspired Room* to help guide you when uncertainty with your decorating process steps in. The helpful hints prod you to gently move forward with your changes but remind you to stay true to yourself and your family. I love that."

Kristy Wicks, *Kristy Wicks* (blog)

"If you are stressing out about how your home looks and feels and want to make it the best it can be, then *Love the Home You Have* is the book for you. It doesn't matter if you live in a tiny basement apartment or a grand, 5,000-square-foot home. The ideas and tips Melissa shares can be done by anyone, in any decorating style, and even on the tiniest of budgets."

Diane Henkler, *In My Own Style* (blog)

"After reading *Love the Home You Have*, I've felt an overwhelming sense of contentment and joy in my home. Melissa has a way with words that really changes the way you think and leaves you with inspiration (true tips to put into place!) to make it a lasting feeling!"

Corinna Henderson, *A Designer at Home* (blog)

"Melissa puts into words so many simple, straightforward, real-life, functional ways to embrace your home. Plus, her ideas include and account for children, pets, and even sometimes husbands! (wink-wink)"

Shannon Fox, *Fox Hollow Cottage* (blog)

"Melissa shares real ideas and simple approaches for working with what you have and moving toward what you really want your home to be."

Laura Putnam, *Finding Home Farms* (blog)

"*The Inspired Room* is a gorgeous book. I know I'm supposed to love the home I have, but I want to climb in and live in this book! Okay, seriously, it's filled with beautiful inspiration but also practical tips that someone (like me) who's not quite as gifted in the decorating department can handle. Melissa is warm, down-to-earth, and exactly the kind of friend you want to come beside you and help turn your house into a home you can love and use to love others."

Mary Carver, author of *Choose Joy*

MAKE ROOM FOR WHAT YOU LOVE

MELISSA MICHAELS

HARVEST HOUSE PUBLISHERS
EUGENE, OREGON

Cover by Nicole Dougherty

Published in association with William K. Jensen Literary Agency, 119 Bampton Court, Eugene, Oregon 97404.

MAKE ROOM FOR WHAT YOU LOVE

Copyright © 2016 by Melissa Michaels
Published by Harvest House Publishers
Eugene, Oregon 97402
www.harvesthousepublishers.com

ISBN 978-0-7369-6317-6 (pbk.)
ISBN 978-0-7369-6318-3 (eBook)

Library of Congress Cataloging-in-Publication Data
Names: Michaels, Melissa, 1967- author.
Title: Make room for what you love / Melissa Michaels.
Description: Eugene, Oregon : Harvest House Publishers, [2016]
Identifiers: LCCN 2015042561 | ISBN 9780736963176 (pbk.)
Subjects: LCSH: Storage in the home. | Orderliness.
Classification: LCC TX309 .M53 2016 | DDC 648/.8—dc23 LC record available at
http://lccn.loc.gov/2015042561

Printed in the United States of America

16 17 18 19 20 21 22 23 24 / VP-JC / 10 9 8 7 6 5 4 3 2 1

Contents

Take It to Heart

Your home should be your sanctuary, your safe haven in this crazy world. It should be inspired by what you love, the memories you've made, and the people you cherish. These lovely sentiments may describe the home you already live in, or at least the place you envision when you picture the dwelling of your dreams. Certainly you want your home to feel comfortable and welcoming, like a warm hug on a chilly day or a refreshing cool drink on a hot summer afternoon.

Whatever our style, our home should be life giving and soul refreshing, a soft spot to land on a hard day and a beautiful place to recharge and rejuvenate. The things we bring into our home can be a reflection of who we are and the life we live.

While a brand-new, empty house may be as inspiring as an artist's canvas, excess white space never feels quite cozy enough until it has memories and creature comforts that invite you to nestle into that place called home. A house filled with curiosities and treasures collected over time, layered with character and expressing personal style, can be so inspiring, endlessly interesting, and warmly charming and inviting.

But somehow in our quest to make ourselves at home, things multiply, and the chaos of living can overwhelm and overshadow the very sense of sanctuary we want to create. We begin wasting precious hours of our life trying to wrangle unwieldy hangers from our overstuffed closets and replacing lost tools because we can no longer find what we need among miscellaneous piles. Soon we become discontented with what we have, and the place we live in is no longer our sanctuary. It's now a storage room where we have become caretakers of stuff and managers of transient things.

If you picked up this book, I'm guessing many of the things you longed for in a home have been lost somewhere deep in the clutter and chaos of day-to-day living. Things you have collected, once loved, or saved just in case have been set aside for someday until they eventually have clouded the vision and hope you once had for the peaceful ambience of your home. I've been there too.

The chaos in our physical world can reflect and even alter the state of our mood, body, mind, and spirit.

I remember a season in my life when I was a young mom and struggled for a short period with debilitating anxiety attacks. While it was difficult to go through some of those dark times, something good came of it that has stuck with me. I became more aware that the state of my outer world was intertwined with how I felt in my inner world, and vice versa. Each part of my life impacted the other.

While I can't always control everything that goes awry in my life, I discovered that there were many things I could do to better manage some things that impacted me. I needed to keep first things first, not only endeavoring to keep my inner soul in order, but also work on refocusing my homemaking priorities and ways of living at home.

I've always loved houses and enjoyed taking care of my surroundings. It was in that season of inner chaos that I began to be more intentional about my habits in my home. If my outer world could affect me so deeply, I was going to invest myself in the things I could better control. I started to make some changes in my approach with my home and life that, little by little, dramatically changed how I felt. My house is still a work in progress, and so am I. But by assessing what worked and didn't work, over the years I've overcome some of my previously ingrained habits and ways of thinking that had kept me perpetually feeling disorganized.

I'm excited to share some of these insights with you on how I started to reset my house and life. I'm sharing not as someone who was born organized, but as someone who has worked hard to overcome the fact that I was not.

In any chaotic season, everything starts to feel overcrowded and out of control, and we cannot see beauty even if it is right in front of us. Clutter suffocates the white space, crowding out the room we need for our souls to breathe and our creativity to thrive. An excess of things will threaten to control your time, taunt you in your sleep, and turn you into a slave of the maintenance of your home and keeper of your stuff. Clutter is a stealer of joy and an enemy of contentment. Your home should breathe happiness into your family's story, not slowly suck the life out of you.

Hope is easily lost amid growing piles of unknown, undone, incomplete projects and "saving it for another day" stuff. You no longer have time for what you love, let alone space to bring what you love into your life.

Yet while your home may not even be close to the peaceful oasis of your dreams, there's hope. It can be more perfect for you if you are willing and ready to step off the crazy cycle of cluttered living and take back control.

If much of your life feels as if it is spiraling into chaos, it's time to take the first steps to regain your sanity. You've probably heard that if you keep repeating the same action over and over again and don't like the result, you need to change your approach. That is true with your home too. You need to get off that merry-go-round and push the reset button.

As you read through this book and discover how to transform your thinking and resulting actions, I hope you will begin to see your home differently. I think you'll find that your ability to transform your home—inside and out, once and for all—is within your reach. Even if you have felt that you are not naturally organized, or if you have trouble making decisions for what to keep or let go of, or if you struggle with homemaking in general, my hope is that this book will encourage you that your home can be transformed.

This is likely not your first attempt at transforming your home.

Don't worry if you have felt inspired for periods of time in the past, only to revert back to the way you lived before. This time you will start to look at your home in a new way and see your life from a new perspective. Once you start this journey toward a more orderly life, you'll never want to go back because not only will your home change in wonderful ways, but you will too.

Perhaps you've read books on decluttering or maybe even spent weeks stressing out over making decisions about what to keep or give away. You might have printed out all the housekeeping checklists and bought all the bins to get organized and tried to follow all the rules. Maybe you've even made a lot of progress but are still not where you want to be. Or maybe you've given up and are hoping for renewed inspiration.

The fact that you've made some attempts to declutter in the past shows that your heart's desire is to find a greater sense of peace in your home. The heart is the perfect starting point. But with that desire you need to add a perspective on the type of changes your heart can embrace. When your heart is on board, you'll more naturally gravitate to new habits as a way of living long after you've highlighted tips and dog-eared the last pages of this book.

If you are like me, you may be pretty good at stuffing things into closets to avoid decisions about what to do with them. Maybe your home actually *looks* okay—certainly to everyone else it appears just fine—but you know that behind closet doors and in storage areas your secret shame is hidden. You have too much stuff, whether it fills your living room or your garage or your closets. You don't feel in control of your home. Instead, your home controls you and your emotions.

There's no shame here, no matter what your home looks like. Whatever your current struggle with stuff is, we are in this together because the state of our home matters. You are my people. Together we will learn to create a home that can transform how we live, enhance how we feel, and will expand our capacity to live out and embrace what we truly love.

These ideas will work for you whether your house is big or small, rented or owned, full of children or just you. We'll discuss methods and come up with potential strategies to rid your home of the clutter. Rest assured, you will make progress in decluttering and organizing your home. But the real goal isn't to plow through quickly to clear out your home and move on with life as it was, only with a view that is a little bit emptier or airier than it was before. There's more to it than empty surfaces and tidy closets.

My desire is to help you nurture a deeper sense of what home means to you so you can live in it with confidence. I want to inspire you to be more decisive so you can make more room for what you really love, both in your home and in the life you lead. My goal is that you will make more room for the things you love as an ongoing way of living, not as a one-time epic decluttering event (although if you can set aside a few months to jump-start this process, all the better!).

If you only remember one thing from our time together, I hope it will be that you become more aware of the decisions you make every day. Those subconscious decisions that keep your home in a state of perpetual disorder can be turned around to help you create the kind of home you dream about.

Creating a home is a journey, and decluttering what you no longer need is only part of the story. I want you to transform the way it feels to be there. I want you to be inspired by what you see around you so you can spend more time *being* who you are and with the people you love, and less time being enslaved to stuff you don't need in your life. I believe how you care for your home can and will inspire your life and impact how you live.

The journey of home transformation should be a gift you are excited to give yourself. You deserve to have a peaceful, orderly, tidy home. Clutter is what weighs you down, distracts, and distances you from the things you dream about. A decluttered home will inspire your life.

Fortunately, while creating a home you really love is a lifelong experience, overwhelming clutter and disorder won't be something you will deal with forever. There will be an end to the sense of this being a drawn-out battle and the beginning of a new way of finding joy at home. Clutter will no longer drag you down and defeat you because you will see it for what it is—an intruder that destroys the serenity of your home.

How about a little visual to inspire you to defeat and outsmart the clutter? Whether or not you are a Dave Ramsey fan, you may have heard the famous financial guru use the phrase *gazelle intensity* to describe the determination by which you should be focused on getting out of debt. Why would an animal like a gazelle have anything to do with succeeding at finances, let alone getting organized?

To survive, gazelles have to outsmart a cheetah, the fastest animal on earth. Cheetahs can accelerate faster than a sports car, so outrunning them seems nearly impossible. But gazelles are smart. They have learned that a cheetah's speed is limited to running in a straight line. A gazelle simply has to bob and weave until the cheetah gets tired and gives up the fight. Who knew a gazelle could be so clever?

So while Dave refers to a gazelle as a reminder of the intensity needed to succeed in getting out of debt and fight off debt collectors, my daughters (who share my love for decluttering) and I have long hijacked the gazelle as a humorous mascot to cheer us on in our mission to outsmart clutter and reach our goals. Whenever we feel as if we have a task that seems insurmountable, we say we have to put our gazelle face on and do this thing.

Life hands us a lot of challenges and curveballs in our journey to create a sanctuary, so we have to be able to navigate our way through the obstacles to get where we want to be. What are we waiting for? Let's get our gazelle face on and do this.

1

Get on the Mission

The difficulty in life is the choice.

GEORGE MOORE

The Things.

We might need these things.
I inherited these things.
I love this thing.
I paid good money for these things.
I just can't decide what to do with these things.
I need to save all the things, just in case.
I remember when my kids wore all these things.
My grandma gave me this thing.
My husband doesn't want me to get rid of these things.
Things broke and I need to fix them. Someday.
I plan to return things.
Someone might need this thing.
These things might fit again someday.
I remember when we bought these things.
These things were so expensive.
I'm hanging on to these things.
I am going to paint or recover these things.

I can't find the other part of this thing.
I might be able to repurpose this thing.
I would use these things, but I can never find them.

Sometimes things start to feel a bit cozier around our house than we intend. Now, I'm all for cozy rooms, but it's quite possible we rationalize our love for so many things and find a way to squeeze them all in so tightly that eventually we will not have room to breathe. (I don't know, but I think breathing just might need to be at the top of our priority list. Wouldn't ya say?)

I remember inviting people over for a party when my husband and I were first married. Moments before our guests arrived at our little condo, I was sweating profusely as I tried to make room for them by cramming all of our clutter, dishes, and piles of dirty laundry into our tiny laundry closet and shutting the door before anyone arrived. The truth is, I wasn't actually trying to make room for the guests. I was trying to hide my secret shame. I had no idea how to keep up a house, and that was the best I could do to make my home reflect what I wanted it to be, a peaceful and welcoming sanctuary.

My stress over piles of stuff wasn't about wanting to impress my guests. I mean, we all have laundry, right? I just wanted the ambience of my home to make it possible for me to enjoy some time with friends. For the life of me, I couldn't figure out how one young couple could create so much chaos.

With a job and a baby on the way, I consoled myself with the fact that I didn't have endless energy to spend working on my home. But I also didn't understand why my home was taking so much of my time and why I had so little to show for the effort. I simply wanted to invite people over, enjoy life, and spend time with people I cared about. I didn't want to spend my time hiding clutter—but more than that, I really didn't like seeing it, either.

Years went by, and as our family grew, so did our belongings. I always felt behind—or at least that I wasn't getting ahead. I'd get one room pulled together, and another would fall apart. I would start projects with big intentions of finishing them, and then trip on them for months before I finally gave up and stuffed everything in a closet.

Thankfully, I stumbled on a thought that changed everything. It was really quite simple, actually. I couldn't believe I hadn't thought that thought before! Once I started to think of it, it made perfect sense.

In order to manage my home and get control of my stuff, I didn't need to work harder or stay up later. I didn't necessarily even need a better household organization manual. I simply needed to start *becoming more decisive about everything.*

Say what? That was it? I didn't just need a better container?

I don't know why it hadn't occured to me before, but my chronic indecision and resulting procrastination was making me feel paralyzed. I was stuck with clutter. I couldn't move ahead on getting rid of it or getting my home better organized because I couldn't even make a simple decision or follow through with the how or what or when or why. Indecision, in so many ways, was preventing me from feeling in control all those years.

If I could learn how to make more efficient decisions and even be more decisive about what really mattered to me when it came to my home, I could be more efficient! It was worth a try, and as it turns out, new habits changed me—and my house.

Make Domino Decisions

You know how it goes. You are really tired at the end of the day, so you decide to save the dinner cleanup or laundry for another day. But tomorrow comes, and you don't want to do it then, either. I mean, do we really ever say enthusiastically, "YAY! I'm so exhausted. I can't wait to do housework!"

Or maybe you keep passing a pile of stuff in a corner of the room, but when you decide to finally do something about it, you are reminded why it's there. It's because you really don't know what to do with it, so you decide to leave it and ignore it. Or you get creative and move the pile to a new place where you don't have to see it every day! Maybe you stuff it in a closet or toss it in the garage for when you'll "have more time" to think about it. Oh, how I relate! Making a decision can be hard, or tiring, or just too much to deal with right now.

Have you ever thought about the fact that by delaying a decision on something, you actually (inadvertently) still make a decision? That sounds confusing, perhaps, but the truth is that each action we take throughout the day at home (even a small or delayed action) will either increase the clutter and chaos or move us closer toward order and beauty.

When we postpone an action or decision about anything, from cleaning up the kitchen to where to put belongings or what we keep or get rid of, we are making the decision to feel overwhelmed later. We probably don't think of it that way in the moment; we actually feel the opposite might be true. If you are like me, you probably think postponing a decision will bring more clarity to the situation or more energy for the task later. And in many decisions we face in life, that reasoning may be true.

But the reality is that when it comes to making simple decisions about tasks and objects around our home, delaying the decision doesn't often contribute to the peace we long for. It actually creates the opposite result.

> *Choosing to be indecisive and not taking*
> *the right action results in a pileup of*
> *indecisive moments we call* clutter.

Let's think about that for a moment.

Look around your home at all the piles and disorder. Look at the surfaces. Open the drawers. Walk around the garage. Look in closets. What is all that stuff? Who put it there? Why is it there? How do you feel when you see all that clutter? Every one of those things that doesn't belong or is in excess likely represents a moment in time where you or someone in your home made a decision in favor of clutter.

Postponing a decision to eliminate clutter *automatically* creates more of the disorder we are trying to escape. Decisions we make about our belongings are like dominoes. They will set off a series of other actions that will either keep our home in *order* or *disorder*. We make the choice with a decision about which way the dominoes will fall whether we intend to or not.

Perhaps postponing decisions is the root of your struggle, as it is mine. I've always been indecisive. When we go out to a restaurant, I take one look at the menu, and if there are more than ten options, I want someone else to decide what I should order (or at least help me narrow down the choices). Too many options induce anxiety. I might ask everyone at the table what they are ordering before I can make a decision for myself. I might ask my husband to order for me. Better yet, I'll find someone to split entrées with me so we can order two things and share them! That way I don't have to decide between two options. I can have my cake and eat it too, so to speak.

I guess I don't want to miss out on the perfect choice when I'm paying for dinner out. I definitely don't want to make a wrong choice, so I feel better leaving those scary and life-altering decisions, such as "the special roast beef dinner or manager's favorite pasta primavera," to someone else. Because decisions like that are big responsibilities.

I mean, now that I've admitted it, doesn't it sound ridiculous? It's just ROAST BEEF or PASTA, right? Either way, I'll eat. First-world dilemmas, I guess.

My indecision isn't limited to food choices. When I travel, I can't decide what to wear. So I bring all the things. All the accessories. All the shoes. I can't decide if I should go casual or dressy, so I bring both. I lug a giant suitcase and carry-on bag with me across the country because I feel I need options and don't want to commit to the wrong choice—yet it's the *options* that do me in. The more I have to choose from, the more indecisive and overwhelmed I am once I arrive at my destination. I usually choose dressy when everyone else chooses casual or vice versa, making me doubt my own judgment. Why is making a firm decision and feeling good about it so hard for me?

Like me, you may have found it difficult to make even simple decisions about what to do with your home. For most of my life, I have struggled with what to buy, what to keep, and what to let go of, so I postponed decisions and created more disorder. Possessions can overwhelm. Choices can paralyze. Decisions can be unnerving.

Even though I was able to run a business and take care of my family, when I used to come face-to-face with a decision about what to do with almost *anything random in my possession*, if no one was around to tell me what to do with it, I became paralyzed.

Perfectionists often struggle with decisions because while they might want a perfect solution, they aren't sure yet what that solution would be, and they may not have time to think about it just then, so they delay action.

Whenever I couldn't decide what to do with something right there on the spot, it felt safer to just *not decide* so I could move on with the day. I would put off tasks like cleaning out a linen closet because I didn't want to deal with all of the decisions that would be involved.

When I first realized that the root of feeling perpetually disorganized at home was my inability to make necessary decisions in a timely matter, it was as if a lightbulb went off in my head. I was causing my own crazy.

For years I had thought an orderly home would naturally be the result of learning the tricks of how to organize things, doing the hard work of color-coding everything, and definitely becoming more efficient at managing all the stuff with the proper techniques for labeling, cataloging, folding, and filing everything in a neat and tidy way.

But as helpful as each of those techniques was, and as hard as I tried, they didn't get me off the crazy cycle of clutter and disorder for long. Before I could truly succeed at creating the home I dreamed about and maintain it for the long haul, I had to start at the *beginning* by laying the right foundation of purpose that stirred my heart so I could become more resolute in my decision making. I had to first be *deliberate* about embracing key principles and goals I had for my home.

Changing my ways and creating a home I loved wasn't just about paring down until perhaps I wouldn't have hardly any stuff at all (although I'll admit at times that sounded tempting!). The truth is, I didn't want to be a minimalist with empty surfaces and barren closets. I love to be surrounded by pretty things and memories of our family and life together. I like clothes. I love dishes and books. I love furniture and accessories. I happen to feel that the existence of a manageable amount of happy things we love will breathe life and soul into where we live.

I want just the right amount of stuff. Not too much, not too little.

Clutter is the result of poor decision making. Many faulty decisions will compound, literally piling up like the clutter they create, causing the chaos you live in. So to break that crazy cycle of clutter, we need to begin by being more decisive about what we invite into our home and life and ruthless about what we need to edit out.

When we start to think differently, we act differently and end up with different results. The key is to start to think in a way that our heart understands, so we can change our results from the inside out.

How can we be surrounded by what we love, but be free of the clutter that weighs us down?

Conquer the Crazy Cycle

In interior decorating, my daughters and I are well aware that it just takes *one wrong decision* to lead everything else in the design astray. When we see a room gone wrong or we make a mistake on a project, we amuse ourselves with the fact that it only took *one false move* for that to happen.

One false move is also what starts off the crazy cycle of frustration, additional expense, clutter, or disorganization. The domino effect is powerful.

Our deliberate or even inadvertent daily decisions can produce an undesirable domino effect that begins to propel us, and our home, into disorder. But what if we were able to harness the domino concept in a way that works *for* us rather than *against* us? What if keeping an orderly home wasn't actually more work at all, but just a matter of making better decisions that will transform our home?

Let's consider this concept in reverse.

If it just takes one *false* move to be the first domino to knock over the rest in a heap of chaos and calamity, even one *positive* move can be the domino to easily inspire habits and successes, knocking others over one by one in the *right* direction.

For someone as indecisive as I was, this was an interesting and freeing thought. My indecision was causing my disorder. I had been making home-altering decisions daily without even realizing it. As long as I could learn to make better decisions about my stuff every day, I would be well on my way to a more orderly and beautiful home.

Domino decisions actually made sense to me, as I had already learned the value of incorporating domino *habits* in my home.

Many years ago, I started making my bed every morning. At first it felt counterproductive. I mean, why make a bed if you are just going to climb back in it at night, right? But much to my surprise, making the bed eventually became a domino habit for me, leading to other housekeeping successes throughout the day.

If I made my bed every day without fail, it was the first domino that led to new positive choices and actions throughout the day. A pretty bed reminded me to open my shades in the morning to let the sunlight in. Once the shades were open, it felt brighter and cheerier in the room, so I was inspired to keep my nightstand and dresser top tidy. With a freshly made bed and clear surfaces in the room, I resisted piling laundry or other stuff all over the bed. Instead, I took a few moments to fold and put things away so my bed could stay pretty all day.

Knowing the success of daily domino habits and how they had changed my daily routines in our home, it made sense to me that being more aware of productive decisions throughout the day would have the same positive domino effect on my home.

Domino habits have become part of the housekeeping routines I practice every day. I don't have to master every task to have a clean home, but the ones I do focus on every day inspire the rest so my home is clean enough on a regular basis. Likewise, the *decisions* I make every day about clutter and possessions become dominoes too and impact my home and life in positive ways.

At first it may seem hard to change when you are used to making decisions based on what feels easiest in the moment, but soon you'll become more focused on your goals and what you want for your home and life, so you'll start to think in a new way. It's simpler than you expect it to be. If you make a decision to let go of even one possession you really don't need, your house will be less cluttered. The positive decision becomes easier!

Soon, as you go to set down that pile of papers on the kitchen counter because you don't feel like putting them in the recycling bin, you'll catch yourself and make a different decision. It might take 2.5 seconds longer to step over to the recycling bin, but you'll be aware that it's a better choice, and it will save you time and stress later. That choice becomes a domino decision because having fewer papers on the counter will affect other decisions in the day. Once you are aware of your tendency to be indecisive, you'll coach yourself through better decisions all day long until they become more natural. Try it!

Here's a simple question to
ask yourself as you go about your day:

Will putting this item here add to the order
or disorder *of this space?*

Make the right domino decision, and you'll find yourself acquiring a more productive habit. Instead of leaving your hair supplies and makeup on the bathroom counter when you leave for work, ask yourself if leaving those items there is contributing to *order* or *disorder*. Take a moment to toss them in the drawer!

Instead of throwing the clean laundry on the floor because you are too tired to deal with it at that moment, get in the habit of pausing to ask yourself if your action will create *order* or *disorder*. If it will only take a few minutes to fold and take it to the proper rooms, deal with it right away and enjoy less chaos later.

While I'm still learning, I've come a long way in how I make decisions. I more quickly recognize those moments when I am making the wrong decision about clutter or housekeeping, and I usually stop myself and make a better choice—or I at least come back right away and correct my mistake. I'll never go back to complete disorder because I know now that the right decisions every day change everything. (And if things do get a little out of hand, good decisions will easily get me back on course.)

Love It

Make tidying the kitchen a more enjoyable daily ritual. Set up a music player or phone so you can listen to your favorite music or enjoy podcasts as you clean. Have a delicious-smelling candle on the counter. Invest in pretty dish towels (fold or roll them in a wire basket on the counter by the sink), and set a brand-new dish-scrubbing brush in a pitcher.

Commit to the Right Mission

Have you ever started a decluttering project at your home, only to find that the mess eventually crept back in? Do you start projects and get partway through them, and then after a while lose interest? Me too.

We tend to get stuck and then disinterested, and we abandon our decluttering and organization projects because we lose sight of what we are doing and why we are doing it. It's hard work! Life gets in the way. Decluttering is not always as rewarding as we need it to be to keep our focus. If we become tired or are too busy or get sick, or a major life change disrupts our progress, it's no wonder we just give up and shove the remaining mess back into the closet. Right? Yeah, I know. I've done that hundreds of times.

So what's your real purpose in decluttering? The truth is, decluttering alone isn't necessarily going to bring long-term happiness. Certainly if you stick with it, you can declutter all the things, and theoretically you'll never have to declutter again as long as you never bring new things into the house. A decluttered house is a worthwhile goal, isn't it? Yes.

But why you are decluttering? Sure, there's a natural joy that will result in seeing an organized desk or a clean kitchen, and that is worth striving for. Celebrate those successes! But then what? What happens next?

I'm sure you are about to slug me because all you wanted to do was set a goal to declutter the house, and now I'm suggesting that you plan what you'll do after that? Decluttering is a goal, but it isn't your *mission*.

When that goal is complete, and the closet is picture-perfect, what does that represent to you?

Decluttering can be like a diet. You can motivate yourself to stick to it long enough to lose your goal weight (or a decluttered closet, as the case might be), and then when you do reach your goal, you celebrate and proclaim you'll never go back to your old ways! You put on that new dress and look great—but often old habits creep back in, the pounds come back, and you have to start over again once you realize you have gotten off track. That's what we want to avoid with our home, right? We want to do this once and do it right.

But we don't want our new aspiration in life to make us so obsessed with perfection that we live in fear of bringing in anything new or restrict everyone to just owning one outfit at a time because, for Pete's sake, we don't want the house or the closet to return to the way it was.

No. Reaching perfection and trying to maintain it isn't the *mission* at all. I think that, as with any other goal in life, long-term success and happiness comes from embracing the bigger purpose so we change from the inside out. We want the outside results to be a reflection of our authentic inner work, so we truly love where we live and don't spend our life trying to figure out how to keep our house looking like a showplace.

What will a decluttered home mean to our life? What might it mean to our family? How will these changes in our perspective and how we manage our belongings influence our thinking, our sense of peace in the home, and success outside the home or in our career? Those questions start to lead us to our real purpose for why we are embarking on this journey.

We need to be thoughtful about our decluttering goals so we know where we are going. What are we doing, and why are we doing it?

While the obvious answer might be that we are doing this to declutter and organize our home so we can have clean closets and surfaces, it's the purpose for those short-term goals that will drive our success over the long haul.

When I started really getting serious about putting my house in order, it was because I was fed up with disorder. But more than that, I was tired of disorder standing in the way of everything I wanted for our life. I was determined to create the environment I wanted for my family and the ambience I needed in order to focus my attention on what mattered to me.

I was tired of just shuffling clutter from one room to the next. I was tired of organizing and reorganizing stuff. I was tired of wasting time on *stuff*! I had a bigger vision for my life. Honestly, clutter just felt like a ball and chain around my ankle. I wanted to make more room in our life for worthwhile things that are intangible, not just more stuff I had to manage.

I wanted a home that was more than just a place for us to organize stuff. I love pretty things and enjoy creating a home that is beautiful to me. But there was also more to it than just wanting a beautifully organized home. I wanted to create the right ambience and find the right balance of stuff so I wouldn't be distracted by clutter, but rather inspired to live a more intentional life.

I wanted to create more space *in between all that stuff* so there was more energy for what mattered most to me. Isn't that what you want too?

When I zeroed in on the bigger purpose of getting rid of stuff and why I was striving to create order out of chaos, something changed in me. I found it easier to have that gazelle intensity because I believed I was going somewhere significant with this. I was no longer a slave to stuff; I was learning to become a master of it. I was empowered to be more intentional every day.

Is your mission to create a perfect house? No. Let's just clear this up once and for all. Your home will never be perfect as long as you continue to live in it. Your goal should not be perfection; it should be to create a home that inspires you to great things. However, setting the bar higher, to better than it has been before, is more likely to bring you success than setting the bar too low. Every decision, no matter how small, will either steer your home toward your goals or away from them. A mess distracts you; tidiness frees you to create the perfect home for you.

Here are some questions to ponder and perhaps journal about as you start to develop your own vision and sense of home:

- What do you really love but feel you never have enough time for?
- Describe your ideal home. What would it feel like?
- What words describe what your home feels like now?
- In the long term, what do you envision achieving in your life?
- How might the state of your home prevent or distract you from success in other goals?
- What inspires you to be happy at home?
- What kind of setting brings you peace?
- What colors feel energizing or soothing to you?
- Does your home reflect your style?
- What is one source of frustration you experience due to clutter?
- What activities bring laughter to your home?
- What would your life be like if your home was always clean and organized?
- What excuses do you seem to make over and over again when it comes to the state of your home?
- If you could start over with a clean slate, which room or closet would be the first you would want to see completely decluttered and beautified?

As you become more aware of what you love and what makes you happy at home, what inspires you to live out your dreams, and what makes you more aware of how your home might impact your life, it will become clearer to you what *you don't want* to invest in.

Do It Now

Keep track of your home goals, daily habits, and home inspiration with a three-ring notebook and plastic sleeves. You can also use folders to keep track of your inspiration photos, home goals, notes, and progress. Find downloads at makeroomfor whatyoulove.com.

I can pretty much bet you don't love disorder or clutter if you are reading this book. There is no doubt about it. Clutter makes functioning efficiently more challenging and makes maintaining your home more costly and time consuming. But imagine a space to breathe and relax in, to be surrounded only by people and things you truly love. That's inspiring, isn't it? That's the kind of house most of us truly dream about.

Your home should be a unique reflection of you and the family you love, and in order to design that space, you have to be honest with yourself about what kind of home you want to create and what it will take to get it.

What is standing in the way of the home you dream of?

Set goals for your home that will inspire you so you can become an effective decision maker in what matters most to you. In turn, you'll make more room for what you really love.

Set Foolproof Goals

If your home is starting to reflect to you that YOU must be a failure, don't let it discourage you with the lie that you are incapable of a beautiful, orderly home. Your home may feel like a failure if it's a disaster right now, but there's hope for you and your home. I know there is, and to help you along the way, I can let you in on my little tricks to make this process easier.

When I was finally fed up with disorder and wanted to transform my home top to bottom to be a peaceful retreat for my family in every way, I knew I needed to make some specific changes.

But before I found the right map, the road ahead felt so overwhelming. I didn't even know where to start. There were too many options! I thought I was too busy for progress. I couldn't decide how to proceed, so I procrastinated. I put off decisions until I had time to figure out the right plan and the perfect solutions.

Even attempts I DID make seemed to stall when the momentary thrill of the idea of organizing ALL THE THINGS ended. I needed a plan that would keep me going and help me to make the right decisions when I was tempted to revert to my old ways.

The reason why most of us fail at achieving our goals is not our lack of enthusiasm for them; it's that we don't have an actionable plan to get us there. It's clear our daily decisions are linked to our results. Think about these scenarios:

- When you can't find your keys or your shopping lists or your shoes because you didn't put them away, your day gets off to a rough start.

- You become cranky and crabby when dishes pile up in the sink. You are just too tired to wash all the crusty dishes from last night, so you go out to dinner three nights in a row and face those dishes for days on end.

- You want to redecorate, so you buy some new accessories. When you get home, you are flustered because you don't know where to put them. They end up collecting dust on a random table or in a closet with other things you don't know what to do with.

- You aren't able to find time for yourself or things you really love because you are too busy trying to keep up with a perpetually cluttered and messy home.

- You buy $60 worth of craft supplies, and you never find time for crafting. Soon you realize you have collected enough craft supplies on your desk to open a small craft store, so you stash it somewhere out of the way. When your kids need craft supplies for a school project, you are

pumped to finally have a use for all that glitter. Unfortu-
nately, now you can't find it for the life of you, so you have
to buy another bottle.

- The piles of dirty clothes on the floor are just too overwhelming, so you feel you have to go shopping for something new to wear.

- You leave a stack of random things on the counter, and it
  multiplies when you aren't looking. Clearing off the piles
  later steals time away from your weekend.

Because our own choices are responsible for the disorder in the
home, we need to get ourselves out of this fix!

I think of this as my foolproof cheat sheet for setting home goals
because it's SMART! Smart, just like a gazelle, right? You may have
heard of this acronym before for goal setting. I love it because it takes
some of the mystery out of how to get from point A to point B.

We need to set goals that are:

S — Specific

M — Measurable

A — Achievable

R — Realistic

T — Time Limited

When I'm feeling all wishy-washy and indecisive about what to do
next, it's so helpful to have someone else boss me around! In this case,
my little cheat sheet gets me headed in the right direction every time.
I hope it will help you too! Our goals need to be *specific* (get rid of old
sweaters rather than just clean out the closet), *measurable* (I want to
pare down to only five sweaters), *achievable* (a goal you can actually
accomplish in the time frame you have), *realistic* (don't set a ridiculous
goal), and *time limited* (set a timeline for steps and completion).

Let's say you want to start making better decisions in the area of clutter prevention around your house. You can create a SMART goal for that! Your goal should be something like this: Every day this week, I will clear my desk of clutter at the end of the evening.

That is a SMART goal because it is specific, measurable, achievable, realistic, and time limited.

Now let's say you really love decorating for Christmas, but you no longer enjoy heading up to the attic because you are so overwhelmed by the amount of decorations you have accumulated over the years. Your dream is to pare down and organize. This may seem like a daunting project you want to put off as long as possible, but creating actionable steps will help you achieve your goal. To take action on our goals, we use "reverse engineering," which is simply putting together the steps to the goal as a map to reach your destination.

First, let's set a SMART goal: *By Sunday night, I want to organize my holiday decor into just three bins by getting rid of everything I don't love or use.*

Now that I have a SMART goal, let's map out the action steps to achieve it:

1. Friday afternoon, I will bring all of my holiday bins to the living room and empty them in the middle of the floor.

2. I will set up three areas: one for things to give away, one for things I want to keep, and one for trash.

3. I will go through each ornament and decoration, keeping only what I still love and actually use and setting aside the rest to give away.

4. By Sunday afternoon, I will organize what I want to keep into no more than three bins, putting all three bins back into the attic. The empty bins will be stacked in the garage.

5. I'll take the trash out to the recycling area, and the items to give away will go immediately to my car to be dropped off Monday at the women's shelter.

By committing to being more decisive and more deliberate in our daily actions, we can start to transform our home into the one we dream about.

Now that you will be more aware that indecision every day invites disorder into your home, it's time to make some goals to kick the chaos out and make more room for what you really love!

What is a SMART goal you could work on this week?

Do It Now

What is one area of your home you've neglected because you just haven't yet committed to making decisions for that space? Let go of trying to find the perfect solution and just commit to a simple one! Take a small step forward with the time, money, and resources you currently have.

Pause, Reflect, and Act

Make Room

What is your mission? Brainstorm a list of reasons why you want to make changes in your home. Go deeper than the fact that you are just tired of clutter. What will a cleaner, tidier, less-cluttered space mean to your life? What goals might you be more inspired to accomplish? Write your reasons on a piece of paper and save it to inspire you.

Let It Go

What is "one false move" you've been making every day that sets off a crazy cycle for the rest of the day or week? Make a list of some unproductive domino habits you need to change. Perhaps you've been leaving dishes in the sink, not making the bed, leaving laundry in baskets, or putting piles of mail or papers in random places in the house. Let those habits go and see the difference!

Home Love Habit

Get in the habit of asking yourself this key question every day. (Perhaps type it out and tape it to every room in your house until it becomes ingrained in your thinking!) "Will putting this item here add to the *order* or *disorder* of this space?"

2

Live Beautifully

The beauty is in the walking—
we are betrayed by the destinations.

GWYN THOMAS

Whether you live in your very first place or you've been making a home in many places for years, it's your attitude about your house, the one you live in right now, that matters. What you invite into your life and choose to have around you should inspire you, and your everyday investment in the place in which you live will connect you to it on a deeper level. As your surroundings begin to inspire you and reflect who you are and what you love, you will sense your house evolving into your home.

There are so many ways to invest in a home and make more room for what we love, but to find that connection between what we love and what we see around us, we have to be observant, both to the house itself and our own personal preferences for how we want to live in that space. Creating a beautiful home requires paying attention to the smallest details. Each color we select, every texture we prefer, and subtle nuances, such as the lighting or scent, will impact how we feel to be at home.

It should be no surprise to us that a home overrun by clutter and disorder is unsettling. There is an intrinsic connection between what we see around us in our home and how we feel to be in that space. When there are many projects or random objects that have been left unattended and disorganized, they will make us feel scattered, behind, or out of control. Disorder begins to influence us in both subtle and rather significant ways.

When you look at a magazine and see a beautiful room, you might be able to confidently say, "I think this room is beautiful." You might point to the colors, the fabrics, the light coming in the windows, the finishes, the flooring, or the countertops. Now look around your own home. What do you see in the room you are in right now? Do you see this room as beautiful? You may notice disconnection between what you see and your preferences for style or colors. And I'm guessing your eyes probably go directly to random clutter scattered throughout the room or piled up on surfaces. If you open your closets, they might be filled to overflowing with things you once felt you needed but no longer represent your life right now. Spaces that are too full or filled with the wrong things make us feel as if we have no room left to invite in what would inspire us right now. We begin to feel trapped with what we have and paralyzed from moving forward.

Yet ridding our home of all imperfection is not only unrealistic, it's not something we should strive for. Homes are most beautiful when they are fully lived in and loved on, don't you think? The surface of the table worn from many family dinners, the party invitations tacked on the family calendar in the hall, homework spread out on the coffee table, the dogs' bowls surrounded by scattered Puppy Chow on the floor, and the coats on the hooks in the entryway ready to be worn are each an obvious sign of the love we have for where we live and the people in it.

A perfectly designed but sterile house is missing signs of life that tell us this home is a true haven where people live rich and meaningful lives, rather than a showplace left empty to impress. A house is really not a home until it reflects the life that is lived and cared about within the walls, exuding the warmth and personality of the people inside.

But a home filled with clutter and disorder tells a different story than we want to share. We might have a sign on our front door to fore-warn our guests that says, "Excuse our mess. We live here," but if the stuff we have piled up in our home isn't truly enjoyed or treasured—if it's stuff that has sat unloved and unused for days, weeks, months, or years—then it isn't representing our life or who we are.

Stuff in our home needs to be used regularly and truly loved and cared for if it's to become a beautiful reflection of who we really are.

Determine What Is Beautiful to You

If you feel that your home really doesn't represents your style right now, or you feel that the wrong stuff is taking over and crowding your personality, it's time to rethink and reclaim your home to make it beautiful to you.

Our goal is to find a style and way of living that inspire us in our current season of life, something that will awaken in us feelings of contentment with where we are and even inspire the direction in which we want to go. To create that space, we should be in tune with what we find pleasing to our own eye, whether or not it's what appeals to others. You might be more comfortable with a home that features perfectly updated and current colors and furnishings, or you might love that gathered-over-time look, or a mix of both. It's your home, so embrace what you love and what makes you feel truly at home.

We don't all feel comfortable with or as stirred by the same elements of design. You may be inspired by a lot of color, decor, and accessories and feel energized by it all, and someone else may feel jarred and uncomfortable in that space. What we surround ourselves with in our home will be a matter of personal taste.

The same is true for how much stuff we have or how organized our home is! The goal is to see beauty in what we create around us. You might need to train your eye to recognize what is beautiful to you by paying closer attention to what inspires you.

How can you train yourself to know what you really want? It's hard to move forward when you feel stuck where you are. It can be hard to imagine your home looking like anything else than what you see in front of you. Believe me, I get stuck too! So to get past what our home looks like at this very moment, we have to find inspiration.

To give myself a creative nudge, I search for a pretty space that will fill me with hope. I love to find a photo that inspires me for each room or closet I want to get organized. An image reflecting a room of order and beauty can help me to zero in on my goals for my own space. Rather than being discouraged by a room that seems out of reach, I will study the image to learn a few things about why that room appeals to me. What can I take away from that space to apply to my own home on my own budget?

When you pore over a magazine or scour Pinterest, do you consider what styles you like, what colors inspire you, what textures soothe you, and what you find beautiful? Look at how the space is arranged and consider how much is in it. Start a list to define for yourself what you feel is essential to your home and what being organized looks like to you so you can find a style that is just right for your family.

Do It Now

Look through photos of rooms or organized spaces you love for inspiration, and tear out or print and gather them in your home notebook. Or, if you have a Pinterest board, make a board to pin organized room inspiration photos. Put captions with how you could apply things you like to your own space.

As you study what appeals to you and even find creative inspiration from others, you will discover that it's easier to decide what you want to keep and what to remove because you'll become more confident in your goal.

Making room for what we love really isn't as difficult as we may fear.

We can easily be paralyzed at the possibilities and the projects ahead, but it helps to have a vision for a home that is cozy, not cluttered; comfortable and charming, not chaotic.

Identify What Clutter Is and Isn't

For your home to really reflect who you are, you need just the right amount of stuff. Not too much, not too little. The more discerning you are about what you perceive as beautiful, the more decisive you'll be about everything you have in your home. It's hard to know what to keep and what to let go of when you really don't know what you love or find attractive. As you become more confident in embracing real beauty in your home, you'll be less tempted to keep unnecessary clutter.

While it may seem easy to tell yourself "only keep what you find beautiful," in practice that isn't always as simple as it sounds. Even if you are in tune with your taste and style, there are many things in your home that might be hard to determine if they add beauty or not.

I think it helps to ask what might seem like a fairly obvious question because it has a surprisingly unclear and confusing answer depending on whom you ask:

What exactly is clutter?

The dictionary defines clutter as a large amount of things that are not arranged in a neat or orderly way, a crowded or disordered collection of things.

While I sometimes try to see everyday clutter on our surfaces as beautiful because it represents that people I love are in the house, the truth is that if I have a *large* amount of things that are not arranged in a neat or orderly way, and it has been that way for many days, I'm over it. If my home is a crowded or disordered collection of things, it isn't going to feel beautiful because a measure of order represents beauty to me. We can have people and activity in our house without being hoarders or slobs, so clutter doesn't have to equal happiness and beauty.

Clutter represents things that are in excess, unloved, forgotten, or simply in the wrong place. Clutter isn't even limited to junk! Interestingly, even the wrong colors can be perceived in our mind as clutter. Think about this. If you feel most at peace surrounded by shades of blue, and your home has a rainbow assortment of red accessories mixed in, you may feel unsettled and not even realize why. The red can feel misplaced and out of order.

If your color palette doesn't flow naturally through your home, you may feel as if your home is in disorder because you perceive the colors as not arranged in an orderly way. It may feel hectic, or that you have too much stuff, when it may be in part that you would just feel better surrounded by a more unified color palette that flows through the room or the entire house.

When clutter of any kind takes over a room, it causes stress, frustration, and a feeling of being out of control. Clutter tells us we are indecisive, perhaps even fearful, because we've invited disorder into our life. No wonder it makes us feel unsettled.

Maybe you look around at all you've acquired in your home and feel an emotional attachment. You see clothing, belongings, or furnishings that have been with you through memorable experiences, both good and trying. If you think a little more about what you see, you will probably notice quite a few decisions that you now regret or at least question. You probably see things you've already invested in that still work for you, but if you are honest with yourself, you see many things you don't love or use that are just taking up space. You may even be able to see a lot of potential for beauty in your space if you can look beyond all the stuff!

So while the happy disarray produced by day-to-day life can feel beautiful in small doses, true clutter is not beautiful. When clutter is defined as excess or too much in disorder, I start to understand why I don't find beauty in the clothes I left overflowing from suitcases that have been stacked on the floor for weeks. Those suitcases may have been a beautiful sight for a day or two as I reflected on the happy experience of travel, but when I don't attend to them soon after I arrive home, they cross over into clutter because they perpetuate a lack of organization and order.

Love It

Is your bedroom a place you consider to be beautiful? Your bedroom should be a retreat. It's worth it to get the ambience of this space just right because you spend so much of your life in this room. What do you envision when you picture your favorite place to retreat? How could you incorporate colors and elements that inspire you? Make it a priority for this space to be as appealing as possible so you'll look forward to spending time there dressing, resting, and dreaming!

I enjoy rearranging accessories on my console table. While I do love a clear surface in a room, too many empty surfaces make me feel unsettled, as if I just moved in. I find beauty in shapes, patterns, and colors, so adding accessories is a way for me to experience more beauty.

But too many accessories cross over into clutter if I can't keep them dusted or they aren't arranged in a pleasingly ordered way. How many accessories you keep or how you arrange them is up to you. No accessory police force is out there ready to hand you a ticket for improper numbers of accessories. This is where beauty will be in the eye of the beholder. If you find beauty in what you see, you have enough space to keep things so they are easy to organize and use, and you don't feel you have become a slave to caring for your accessories, just enjoy them.

The secret to embracing your own style is to become so aware of what you find beautiful and inspiring that you can quickly spot clutter and deal with it decisively. As you begin to reflect more on what you really love and what represents your style now, you very well might decide that most of what you have feels like clutter. You may want to be expressing yourself in a new way and not feel stuck in a time warp. Removing what no longer holds value to you or contributes to your sense of home can be a freeing experience.

Your budget may not allow you to express your personality quite as fully as you might dream right now, but that is actually a blessing in disguise. If you rush out to express yourself, that will distract you from the mission. You'll find more success if you take your time, focusing more right now on what you can take away to reveal the beauty already there.

Create Authentic Action Steps

Chances are, your home and family dynamics are different than mine. Your style will likely be different too. How does your family live in your home? Where do they spend their time? Where do kids do their homework? Where do you watch TV or play games? What are your family's hobbies? Do they read or play instruments? Do you entertain? First and foremost, the focus is to create a home that works for your family and provides the surfaces, supplies, storage, and furnishings you need to live well.

Create a little floor plan or list for each room and identify what activity takes place there. How is each room used? How could it be used more effectively? What could you enjoy more in each space if the rooms were utilized more effectively? Contemplate what furniture would be or is useful for storage to make the most of that space.

To succeed in making room for what we love, we need to commit to a plan that will work for us and make the most of the spaces we have. That's what I love about reverse engineering goals for improving the home. Your ultimate vision for your home will set the goal you are longing for, and your own determination to get there from where you are will offer you the action steps.

Being more decisive about what you need in your home and what you find beautiful is an important step in your progress. The more decisive you can be, the less clutter you'll face. The more specific you are about your goals and more decisive you become about your style, the more obvious it will be when something doesn't fit.

To get to know ourselves better, we have to be honest about the life we lead in our home, not just the dream life we imagine but isn't realistic for us in this season.

What are the chances you'll tackle a DIY project in the near future? You may aspire to be a DIY'er, but are you in practice? I love DIY, but the reality of my schedule and past failures provided me a clear answer. I wasn't going to tackle a DIY project if the material for it had been sitting around longer than two weeks. I needed to become ruthless about ridding my garage and rooms of extra chairs that needed reupholstering. I just said no to hoarding pieces that could be really pretty if only they were painted. I either embraced the beauty of items in their existing state or found them a new home.

I had more room when I finally admitted I wasn't a DIY diva. If something wasn't already beautiful to me as it was, it became easier to just say no to keeping it in hopes that a future project would change it. Once I knew what I was willing to invest my time and effort in, I was able to declutter with greater ease. I became decisive about what I knew to be true. "If this isn't beautiful right now, and I'm not going to be the one to make it better anytime soon, I should let it go to someone else." "If I don't have the time to host a garage sale or place the items on Craigslist this week, I won't likely make it a priority next week either, so I should drop them off now at a donation center."

Getting to better know myself and my style helped me to create definitive statements about what I found beautiful and what I didn't, what projects I was likely to complete, and which ones I would likely put off forever. This determined what I should keep and what I should let go.

When we don't know our style, we can inadvertently create more clutter by making wrong decisions.

For instance, there were times when I wanted to improve my home, so I would head to the local home store and load up on new accessories. Perhaps you find yourself doing that too. Yet for me, all that was really accomplished by shopping was more stuff in the house. Getting more stuff wasn't the effect I was after.

As I became more confident in what I really loved and what would contribute to our home, I became better at decision making. I was able to list appropriate action steps for future projects or purchases. Buying more accessories on a whim wasn't the right decision. What I really needed to do was to unify what I already had by streamlining my color palette and getting rid of accessories that didn't contribute to my style. Once I completed those steps, I had a clearer picture of what was needed to complete the room and could shop if necessary.

Room by room, item by item, I started to create more beauty and order one decision and action step at a time.

A fun way to dive into this process of refining your home is by taking away what doesn't bring you joy or contribute to the look you want. Reflect back on your room map. What do you use this space for? What should it be used for? What makes sense in each room and what doesn't?

Of course, always start with removing the trash and dirty dishes or anything else that obviously is out of place. Then give yourself small goals, such as reducing your accessories by 50 percent in each room. Remove what doesn't reflect your style. If your rooms are very cluttered, go through again and remove another 50 percent. Each time you should be able to breathe a little easier and pare down to what is most beautiful to you.

Beauty is found in the way we live and in those spaces we truly live in, so finding that authentic way of expressing yourself and your style is what will bring you more peace and satisfaction with what you have.

Surround Yourself with What You Love

You might have heard advice that suggests the house of your dreams is as simple to achieve as keeping only what you love or what makes you happy. A lifetime of memories of travel, children, special occasions, milestones, and achievements can be represented among our favorite treasures. Things we've collected through the years tell our story and create a home rich with meaning and the history of those who live there.

Yet there may be many things you own that make you happy but you really don't have room for. There may be many things you don't need that you are tempted to bring into your home because you think they are beautiful. And there may be many things in your home you don't really love but can't afford to replace or do without right now.

How does one decide what to buy, keep, or let go of?

In *Steal Like an Artist*, Austin Kleon says that "artists don't hoard indiscriminately; they are collectors." There is a fine line between the two sometimes, don't you think? Do you have drawers filled with beautiful things you love but rarely ever use? Do you have trouble finding things you love because your closets are overflowing? Artistic people often become collectors of beautiful things even if they don't see themselves as hoarders of those items. But every year more beautiful things come into our possession. We have more art, more accessories, more memories, and more furniture.

Being surrounded by things we love is wonderful, but if we have too many things, we need to make room for what we love most in this season of our life and only hang on to things we truly treasure.

A turning point for me was realizing that while I may have classified much of what I owned as beautiful to me in some way, all together they weren't beautiful at all. They were chaotic. Managing stuff (even beautiful stuff!) added to my stress level. Once I started looking at what I owned and how effectively it all worked as a whole, I realized that too much of even beautiful things created a not-so-beautiful experience.

If you are a musician, you'll appreciate this analogy. (Even if you aren't, I think you'll understand the point.) If you have an entire orchestra available to you, each instrument needs to play its part just as it was designed to, on key, in harmony, and coming in at just the right measure. If one instrument is off, the whole piece will sound wrong. So to create beauty in my home—to surround myself with things I truly loved—I needed to create harmony as a whole. A closet crammed full of beautiful accessories is not beautiful to me any longer, but if I have a beautiful composition of vases lined up on a shelf to use and enjoy? That is beautiful.

Remember, you need to assess what you love right now and what is authentic to your way of living in this season of your life. If your home is too small for what you own, too much stuff will overpower the space you have. We happen to be book lovers, so we have stacks of books everywhere and wouldn't have it any other way. Perhaps my house would feel too cluttered for some, but books are meaningful to us, so they enhance our rooms. I'm not sure one can have too many books in a house, but, of course, how many of anything you have is always a matter of personal taste and honoring the space you have.

You know how word gets out that you have a collection of some kind and pretty soon everyone is giving things to you in that theme? Take geese for example. At some point my mom must have mentioned liking geese. Or probably she never said anything of the sort. She just happened to pick up a few geese accessories one day. Big mistake. One decision leads to another, you know, and the first decision to add geese definitely proved to be one false move. Now the geese were multiplying. Some of them had bows around their necks. Some of them had baskets in their beaks. Some wore bonnets. There were porcelain geese hooks that looked as if they were poking their heads out of the wall. Every one of them probably represented some kind soul (bless their heart) who thought they knew my mom well enough to know she was a geese lover.

How many geese will be too many in your space? That is something only you can decide. No matter how many you have collected or how much they are worth now, if you no longer love something (or never did), it's time to let them fly away.

What you keep will determine your style, so don't keep things that don't add meaning or value to your home. Your story is told in what you are surrounded with, so make sure each piece you have and keep is fulfilling a role that makes sense.

You may eventually find a need to add furniture pieces to what you already have in order to create more functional storage or comfort, but don't worry if your budget doesn't allow you to be fully surrounded yet by things you love. The goal isn't so much to have a home full of things that make you giddy (that sounds like a visual headache, doesn't it?), but rather a home that functions well and feels comfortable.

You can find more decorating ideas and tips for how to add furniture, color, and texture in my book *The Inspired Room* and on the blog by the same name. The key in making more room for what you love is to give yourself time to add needed furniture pieces to your home. Your home and budget will thank you for not rushing right off and filling it with things you love, but rather letting it evolve authentically. Enjoy discovering the perfect pieces. Take time browsing flea markets. Experiment with new furniture arrangements. Reupholster things you love that have seen better days. Your home doesn't have to be complete today. You'll love it even more if it comes together over time.

To be better prepared to find things you love, measure each room and the spaces you have to fill. If you need something to store dishes in your dining room, make note of how wide, deep, and tall the furniture should ideally be. Put the measurements in your phone in case you think you've stumbled on the right piece!

As you wait for more suitable furnishings, you'll be able to become creative in putting together a room you'll love so much more when it is more efficiently organized. Look for pieces you already have around the house that can serve an organizational purpose right now. Maybe you have an old TV cabinet that can hold linens and plates in the dining room. It might not be the perfect size or look, but it can help you to get more organized while you wait. Perhaps you have an old nightstand that could be refreshed with paint to hold all the supplies you need in your office.

Look around your house. What could you use in a new way? You can always replace a piece later with something that works better for you or that you love more, but the surprising result of decluttering and creating function and order first is your home will feel more beautiful!

Five Ways to Streamline, Simplify, and Display What You Love

1. Practice restraint. Just because you have a lot of cute objects and collections doesn't mean you need to have them all out at the same time. Create seasonal displays of things you love, rotating collections so you don't overwhelm your space.

2. Group like objects together. Find a common theme to your accessories and group items together for display rather than spreading accessories throughout the house. For instance, if you collect sailboats, pull them all together on one display shelf for a big statement. Mismatched or unrelated accessories strewn around tabletops can become a more streamlined collection if you arrange them together on a shelf with a common color theme.

3. Streamline and unify. When you display items on a tabletop or wall, keep the items closer together but equally spaced out in the middle third or half of the wall or furniture piece rather than spread out across the entire surface or wall. This will bring more unity to the display and a more streamlined look.

4. Everyday on display. Consider freeing up storage space by putting a collection to use. Perhaps you have a collection of pretty teacups. Use them in drawers to organize jewelry or divide hair ties. You'll be delighted to see your pretty cups every time you open the drawer, and now you can more easily find those little accessories you enjoy too.

5. Breathing room. Your eye needs places to rest for your accessories to be fully appreciated. Don't fill every surface in your home with trinkets. Allow some breathing room so your collections can be enjoyed, not be lost in the clutter! If you are feeling unsure where to draw the line between cluttered and classy, empty your tables completely and give yourself some time to cleanse your visual palette. See how little you can put back while still enjoying the space.

Pause, Reflect, and Act

Make Room

Make room for your authentic style to shine through. What pretty things will you invite in to inspire you when you kick out disorder? Perhaps you visualize a new, streamlined color palette or more orderly tabletops filled only with accessories you love. Visualize what you want to invite in and search for inspiration photos for what you imagine.

Let It Go

What excuses have you been giving for why your home isn't beautiful to you? Let them go, one by one. Do you tell yourself you can't afford a pretty house? Get creative and make it happen over time, starting today. Do you tell yourself you are too busy? Un-busy yourself for 15 minutes a day to tidy a space. Do you tell yourself other people are responsible for the mess? Give yourself the gift of sanity and claim one room to beautify even if no one else cares as much as you do.

Home Love Habit

When clutter in a room is crowding out your vision for your home, a new habit can transform it. What new habits could you practice every day to show your home some love? Start with one and build from there.

3

Choose Simplicity

Our life is frittered away by detail...Simply, simplify.

HENRY DAVID THOREAU

I n *The One Thing* by Gary Keller, he describes what I find to be
secrets to simplification in life as "going small" and "ignoring all
the things you could do and doing what you should do. It's recog-
nizing that not all things matter equally and finding things that matter
most. It's a tighter way to connect what you do with what you want.
It's realizing that extraordinary results are directly determined by how
narrow you can make your focus."

Going *small* is the opposite of what we think to do when we
are striving for results. Isn't life all about GOING BIG or GOING
HOME? Do people with an organized, clean home spend more time
on housekeeping or have a longer to-do list to check off each day than
everyone else? Isn't a sign of success the resulting happiness we will
experience if we have more clothes, more toys, more gadgets, more
house, more stuff?

We do need to learn the art of more, but not in the ways we might
think. What we really need is to focus more on things that matter to us,
and to do that we have to become gazelle-focused on eliminating more
of the things that don't. Think about the last time someone asked you
how life was going. Did you tell them, "I'm good! I've been really busy!"

Busy has become our default way of living. But if we were able to look more closely at our home and life, we would find simple ways to delete, edit, and declutter what isn't essential to make more room for what is.

Think of something you wish you could make room for in your life. Exercise? Time with your kids? Hobbies? Spiritual pursuits?

How can we be MORE selective about what we add to our life and be MORE intentional about what we do with the time and space we have?

To succeed in simplifying our life and home, we have to first embrace what less will mean. We need to visualize having less stuff as making more room for what we love. Isn't that what we really want? A life surrounded by what we love and what inspires us?

> *Remember the key: Have just the right amount of stuff. Not too much, not too little, but just what you need to have a home you love.*

Reduce Decision Fatigue

Have you heard of decision fatigue? The minute I was introduced to this concept, I not only knew I related to it, but that understanding it would change my life. Decision fatigue is a recognized psychological condition in which productivity suffers because you become mentally exhausted from making too many decisions. HELLO! That's me. Maybe it's you too.

When I'm on overload, I cannot handle one more decision. I shut down. I start making dumb decisions because I don't have the energy to think things through. I have suffered from decision fatigue through everyday events and big changes in my life, which only makes my tendency to postpone decisions more complicated. Not only do I have to face more decisions every day, I'm often still recovering from having to make taxing decisions months or years before.

Moms raising growing children should be able to relate to this type of overload on our brain, and so should anyone who has taken on a new challenge in life, such as going to college, planning a wedding, applying for a job, starting a business, or buying a house. Big decisions are a part of life if you are ambitious and have a zeal for living.

Even when we aren't facing a big life change or event, most of us are bombarded daily with seemingly small, inconsequential decisions our parents or grandparents may not have even dreamed of making. We have so many choices and options at our fingertips. What colors or styles will we wear each day of the week? What should we eat and at what restaurant? Where should we go for entertainment? What brand of cereal is healthy, and which one is likely to cause health problems? Should we eat grain-fed beef? What shade of white should we select from the thousand paint chips available to us?

With innovation, many of us in this generation have introduced many Internet-connected devices to our daily activities. We have our iPhone, our iPad, our computer and laptop, and a Kindle at our disposal. Each one brings with it a learning curve and potential problems we need to solve. If you are like me, you end up at the Genius Bar with 50 other bewildered and overwhelmed customers sitting at the counter hoping for help.

When those devices function as intended, the world is opened up to us. Now we can keep in touch daily (hourly, every waking moment!) with all the friends we like and those we've never met. We can invite them to speak to us as we follow their thoughts and comings and goings, and we can become distracted as we feel compelled to follow the rabbit trail of clicking on every single thing they enjoy too!

We can pick up our phone to research all of the restaurants and products we are interested in to compare reviews from dozens of sources, or we can sit down at the end of the day and face the choice of hundreds of TV shows and movies at our fingertips. We are faced with input to our brain from far too many choices, superfluous information, and a flood of facts even in our downtime. It's more input than our brain is wired to focus on.

My husband was frustrated the other day because his old laptop was giving him the "your startup drive is full" error message, causing nothing else to save. We were frantically dumping old files trying to make more room for what he needed to load. The same thing happens to my email system if I don't delete enough emails. (I'm terrible about deleting emails, but hey, I do like to keep records of important information!)

It should be no surprise that those error messages mirror what our brain, and even our home, is trying to tell us. We are on overload. So many little things rob us of time, energy, and joy. It's time to simplify. Clutter prevents simplification, no matter what form of clutter it is. When we have too much stuff in all areas of our life, including our home, clutter stifles us and prevents us from seeing what it is we already have.

> *The home that is supposed to be our sanctuary, our haven from the chaos outside, is full-to-overflowing with things that drown out the peace we are craving.*

We eventually don't have any more room in our schedule or literal space in our home to breathe. Excess in all areas of our life clogs up all available room, making the experience of each day more stressful and less peaceful. We are so focused on scurrying about trying to keep up the frantic pace that we feel at a loss for how to slow it all down. We have no time or energy left.

I get tired just thinking about all of the clutter we have brought into our life, don't you? Eventually, I realized what I had been doing. I had invited that pace into my life through a series of daily choices I barely even noticed I was making. I started a mission several years ago to simplify everything I could to streamline my life in whatever ways were possible so I could reduce the excess that wore me down. When I invite in too many voices, too many choices, and too many decisions, the frantic pace will eventually lead to breakdowns in my health and home, so I decided enough was enough. I was going to take back my life.

The pursuit of less is becoming more aware of how our choices, belongings, and daily decisions have complicated our life so we can make a change.

What is one thing you could work on to simplify life at home? A good habit to work on is to start making life a little less complicated.

Love It

Let your bed-making ritual be an enjoyable part of your morning. Spritz a linen spray or essential oil blend on your sheets before you pull up the covers. Find special pillows to prop up against your headboard and a beautiful throw to drape across the end of the bed. (If you have pets and kids, find one that is machine washable.)

Offer Fewer Options

Perhaps you pare down to offer yourself fewer options in what you wear or keep in your closet. With fewer choices, every morning you will easily decide what to wear and be able to quickly get ready for the day. You will have less laundry. You will have less to buy to coordinate with all the random items you never wear because you no longer keep random things you don't wear. Less clothing means you have a more orderly closet, so tidying up will be a breeze.

Work with What You Have

Maybe you make simpler decisions regarding home improvement. For instance, you might work within the space you have rather than buying a bigger home or adding on space. Simplification might mean deciding to do more with less space, paring down, and getting organized. While more space can be convenient, it also can add additional expenses, bigger projects, more choices to make, more decisions, more to maintain, more to clean, more to furnish, and potentially more stress.

Plan Ahead

Simplification can occur when we plan ahead. At first it might seem more complicated because we're not accustomed to thinking ahead or doing things before they become urgent, but the pursuit of less in a week may mean we prepared in advance so the rest of the week is more streamlined. Plan to grocery shop just once a week instead of giving it your first thought at six p.m. and then running out feeling frazzled as you try to decide what to eat. If you set aside time to chop and prepare the week's veggies on Sunday afternoon, you'll save time later and likely eat more vegetables and less junk.

Remove Distractions

Perhaps you make the decision to simplify your evening even further by allowing fewer interruptions or distractions at mealtimes. You could require that all cell phones and electronic devices in your home be turned off before dinner. Less reliance on devices might mean more help in making dinner! If no one has alarms going off, texts beeping, or Facebook alerts, you will have fewer interruptions, which will result in more interaction that matters right there at your own table.

Making a few better-thought-out strategies will simplify our day, allowing us to pursue more of what we want in our life, and feel less frazzled trying to keep up with everything else.

Love It

Spend half an hour a day quietly gathering your thoughts. It's amazing how complicated our day gets when we haven't had a moment to breathe deeply and reflect. Clarity shines through silence, so make it a priority to just listen to your heart and mind without distraction. Step off the crazy cycle and get on the path to simplicity, order, and beauty by making time to breathe a priority every day. You can combine this time with doing dishes or laundry or eating lunch or waiting in a carpool line if you are able to focus on something else while mindlessly doing a daily task.

Embrace the Pursuit of Less

I love to go out into the country and just look up at the sky so I can see the stars. Those same stars are in the sky where I live—it's just that the activity and the hustle and bustle of the city distracts from their presence. If we were able to remove the noise, the activity, and the things that dim their shine, we would see the stars more clearly, brightly sparkling against the black sky.

Isn't that the way it is with our home? We get so much stuff that we can't even find what we want, let alone see what we already have. Sometimes what we love is right front of us; we just have to simplify and remove whatever is standing in the way so we can see it with greater clarity. Whether we fully realize it or not, the state of our home and the pace of our life are connected, each one impacting the other. Simplification of both our inner and outer world will allow us to take a deep breath and appreciate more fully what we really value.

Making more room for what we love always has a positive and inspiring outcome, even if the process of letting go feels clumsy and even hard at times. When we are faced with a dilemma or decision about what to do with the time or things in front of us, it will be easier to choose the path of less when we remember that less is really more.

We need to make every effort and take every opportunity to simplify our time, priorities, and belongings. Every decision we make or action we take to have less is an opportunity to increase room in our life and home for what we love.

Do It Now

Simplify your mealtimes and grocery shopping trips. Make a list of five go-to meals your family loves that are easy to prepare in a hurry. Write out a list of pantry items and fresh food needed to make those meals and keep a copy in your wallet or with your shopping list. Each week, assess what you have from the list and replenish when you go shopping so you always have at least five meal options on hand for nights when you are too tired or busy to make something new.

Once you are ready to pursue your gazelle intensity and a passion for simplicity, you might want to make a few changes in your life to make the process less difficult. Here are some ideas for simplifying decisions and reducing what you allow into your life to help jumpstart your mission.

Five Steps to a Simple Home

1. Avoid temptation. When you can, don't go to places that will cause you to buy more stuff to deal with or tempt you with more decisions that will need to be made. Try consolidating shopping lists and trips so you don't make multiple visits in a week. It's amazing how much less you buy and how much easier your subsequent decisions are when you spend less time going into stores.

2. Simplify your daily options and choices. If you are a busy person or struggle with excess clutter, you have too many decisions to make. Why complicate life with unnecessary ones? Instead of keeping thirty outfits in your closet, try to create five you love and use accessories to change them. You'll save daily stress and lots of laundry! Instead of having four sets of dishes in various colors and patterns, keep one basic set in a neutral color and fancy it up with colorful salad plates or glasses. Instead of six extra sets of sheets, own only one or two sets per bed in your home. Wash them in between uses and put them right back on the bed or in the linen closet. Embrace one item that has multiple purposes rather than several specialty items.

3. Commit to making the simplest decision as often as possible. Don't rationalize a choice that makes life or storage more complicated. If you rarely use your food processor, give it away and don't give it a second thought. Don't even consider what you might do with it someday; just let it go. If you find you really do need a food processor on occasion, find a neighbor or relative who will loan one to you. Some decisions might sting for a week, but if you rarely used those items, you'll soon forget what you gave away.

4. Make a daily to-do list and set home goals. Defined vision for your day and home will keep you focused on what matters. When you have a clear task list, you are able to bring less decisions and stuff into your life by focusing on and finishing what really matters to you.

5. When in doubt, throw it out! When you are in the midst of a major decluttering project that may take weeks or months, you don't have time to analyze every possible item. If I'm not sure if I want something or not, it has to become a firm, clear no. I don't even let myself think about who else might want it or how much money I spent on it. If time is of the essence and decluttering is the ultimate goal, off it goes to a charity.

Live Without Baggage

You know how exciting it is when you are packing your bags for a much-needed trip or a move to somewhere new? We might equate baggage with possibilities, freedom, or adventure! But when you live with excess and clutter, baggage of any kind symbolizes that you are not fully embracing the life you already have.

Baggage represents that we are still tied to something in the past or hoping for something in the future that distracts us from fully embracing where we are today. Baggage takes up valuable real estate or adds to the clutter in our home. Many memories we keep from the past or save for the future are treasured and can enhance our life, but so much of what we hold on to doesn't contribute in the same way. That is what I consider baggage. To live in the moment, we need to unpack the bags, stop stuffing things into every available space, and live more simply right now.

Have you ever thought about all of the things you've kept that do not add value to where you are now, but simply take up residence as emotional or mental baggage for a life you do not live today? Or what about all the things you've kept because you can't remember what it's used for, things that were once important but no longer make sense to you? Think about those parts, manuals, and instructions to stuff you may not even own or use anymore. What about everything that is broken and waiting for a repair? Or what about all the things you've kept for some future situation you may never have?

Baggage Slows Us Down

Baggage slows us down (even though we may think we've solved the problem by adding wheels and a handle!). Baggage impedes our progress and ties us to an object rather than giving us the freedom to move about and live our life. I don't know about you, but when I'm hauling a big suitcase across the airport and in and out of taxis, I'm exhausted! It feels like an extra appendage.

Baggage Makes Us Tired

With the amount of luggage I have been known to carry around, I cannot wait to get to my destination so I can set it down. It hurts my arms, my hands, and my shoulders to haul something so heavy around with me. I've tried checking baggage in hopes of traveling lighter, but that only results in my bringing more because I can check a bigger suitcase. I've tried traveling with only a carry-on, and even that is cumbersome to drag down the narrow airplane aisle and stuff in an overhead bin.

Baggage Is a Burden

Baggage always feels like a burden because it complicates our life. For instance, when you move into a new home and see all the stuff you didn't even realize you had rolling out the front door into a moving truck, or when you are bemoaning the extra expense incurred to transport and store it, you will likely feel burdened and weighed down. Baggage is like a ball and chain, something you feel the weight of even if you are not always physically carrying it yourself. Once the moving trucks arrive at your new home, you now feel stressed by how much you have to unload and find a place for.

If you are like many people, the last day of packing and moving out of a house is the worst. Weeks before you carefully packed up your treasures, the things you love and enjoy. By the end of the experience, you are throwing garbage and miscellaneous stuff into trash bags and heaving it into the truck. Right? Why? It's because we have become hoarders of excess. All that excess requires handling, repair, hiding, and washing, and it takes up valuable space. Stuffing our excess in suitcases, bins, or boxes isn't the answer to a more simple life. Lightening our load is the only way.

We want to feel free to enjoy the things we love in our home, not be tied down or burdened by the weight of baggage. Stockpiling baggage from the past or for the future does not add value to you as a person or enhance your home, so why keep it? Take a walk around your home with an eye for what looks suspiciously like baggage. Open your cabinets. Peek in the drawers. Brave the garage. How much baggage you can find? Would you enjoy the idea of carrying any of this stuff with you on a trip around the world? I think not!

Here are a few helpful questions to ask yourself when you are debating what should stay and what should go:

1. Do I feel burdened by keeping these items? Do these items limit my enjoyment of my home or overwhelm my storage space in any way (whether it's the item individually or the combination of ALL the sentimental items causing clutter and stress)?

2. Do I see these items often enough that they are really able to bring me joy? Is there a way to use them so I would enjoy them more?

3. Why do I feel the need to keep this? Is it because I really love it? Is it because it has good memories attached to it? Do I use it often enough to make keeping it worthwhile? Would I feel bad for the person who gave it to me if I were to let it go?

4. Would I buy these things today if I didn't already own them? (If the answer is no, let it go.)

5. Who do these items belong to? If they don't belong to me, why do I let someone else's baggage fill my space?

6. Do I even know why I have these things? (If I can't remember or have to think too hard, it's baggage that will need to find a new home.)

7. Am I holding on to things that are broken? (If I haven't fixed them within a few weeks, chances are I never will. Let them go.)

8. Are these items from my past that are taking up valuable real estate I need for other things? (Good memories can be treasured in ways other than hanging on to physical items. Letting things go doesn't mean the memories aren't special. Find a creative and less-cluttered way to honor that memory.)

Baggage starts with faulty decisions that became dominoes towards disorder. Individually keeping these things may not seem very significant, but the combination of them all causes the chaos. To tackle the baggage you've been carrying around or stuffing into your storage areas, remember that setting SMART goals will help you to make progress.

What area of your home is overrun by baggage? These are smart words from Randy Alcorn: "We think we own our possessions, but our possessions own us."

Love the Simple Life

Many of our decisions to add things we think we need in our home or will enjoy in life are the cause of additional clutter and stress. It's become almost second nature in our culture to think we are going to enhance our life with something new when inadvertently we have made it more complicated.

We've added more debt by buying things we really didn't need, we've created more clutter, we own more clothes, and we bring in more furniture and toys. Then we wonder why we are so disorganized and overwhelmed.

When I started to realize my own tendency to create and invite too much of what I didn't even want in my daily life, I decided to make some changes by paying more attention to what was in my home so I could quiet the pace and chaos of life.

Even though I run a business and have a pretty full schedule, I crave a simple kind of life in my home. Not simple in that I need to get rid of everything I have, sell our car, change my entire color scheme to neutrals, live off the land for our survival, or move to a tiny house or whatever others might view as simple, but simplicity in finding a regular rhythm of life that works for me. I find fulfillment now differently than I used to.

One thing I know for sure is that what might appear to be "the simple life" for one person doesn't necessarily equate to simple for another. That's okay. You have to define simplicity for yourself. For me, simplicity is about being in the moment and embracing life right where I am. It's having more room for daydreaming, solitude, and reflecting. It's simplifying so I have room for simply being present without distraction. I want to make enough room in my house to feel comfortable with things I love to have around me, the type of decorating I enjoy, and the kind of entertaining we want to do as a family. A simple, well-maintained home is more important to me than having so much stuff that I cannot keep up with it all. I need sane space in my house to feel as though I can breathe.

While I'm all for chasing dreams, I think it's important to find a level of contentment with the life we have and what we can control. It can be tiring and distracting chasing after a new kind of adventure, so whenever possible, I crave slowing down and simplifying what I already have as a foundation. It comes down to the choices I make day to day to keep life simple.

What do I do every day that complicates my life? What everyday decisions could I make that would make life more simple or some dreaded tasks unnecessary?

Do It Now

Simplify your morning routine. What is the one thing that happens every morning to cause a little frustration? Is your sink full of dirty dishes? Do you have trouble finding your shoes, or do your kids always forget their homework? Find a simple solution and make the change to streamline your life.

Here is a list of questions that I've found helpful in determining what items should be invited in or removed from our home:

- Is there a simpler option?
- What decision will add the least amount of stress and decision making over time?
- Is this something I actually need in my life right now, in this season?
- If I do think I need it, what might life be like if I didn't have it? Is it a hardship or just a momentary inconvenience to do without it?
- What might happen down the road if I add this item to our life? How long will we have it? How often will we use it?
- Will it likely break in a year or two?
- Will it need maintenance?
- Is this a quality item I will treasure right now, or am I

buying it today just because it seems like a good deal to hang on to for future use?

- Will it cause me frustration trying to learn something new, so might I put off using it because I don't have time to learn new tricks?

- Will there be new activities I need to add to my life as a result of owning this new item (such as, does it require special cleaning, repair tools, extra insurance, new knowledge, experts I will need to call for help)?

- What happens if I lose it or it breaks? Will I have lost a lot of information or money invested?

- Do I have room to display it right now if that is what it is intended for?

- Do I have a convenient and not overflowing place to keep it when it is not being used? What is the likelihood I will actually use it down the road if I put it in a storage area?

- If I break the cost of this item down by how much use and enjoyment I will get out of it, is it worth it?

- What is my track record with similar items? If I'm buying an elliptical exercise machine, what kept me from enjoying the stationary bike and rowing machine I already have, and why will this be different?

- Do I already have this item in the same or a different shape or color? Will life be better with two nearly identical items, or can I make do with just one?

- Is there a simpler way to achieve what I want without owning something new?

- Can this item be borrowed rather than owned?

- Could I appreciate the beauty of this item without owning it and storing it?

Oftentimes we simply haven't weighed the alternatives and out-come of our decisions. We buy without thinking. We start projects on a whim. We make decisions about what to keep based on if we like it and think we have room to store it rather than if we really need it.

A key to remember as we weigh whether or not to bring something new into our life is that it isn't just that one decision. Each decision about what to bring in or let go of becomes a domino decision that will either knock the rest of our life toward simplicity or excess.

As I let go of stuff I don't need to make room for what I love, I delight in the resulting joy I receive from the sense of order, beauty, composition, and usefulness from that which remains. Letting go of things brings me more freedom to be who I am today. When I create more room, what I'm left with delights my eye when I see it rather than adds frustration to my day. That sense of order gives hope, brings more possibilities, and makes room for more of what really matters in my life.

Pause, Reflect, and Act

Make Room

Create breathing room in your home through design decisions, simplified lifestyle choices, and careful attention to what you keep. How are your schedule, your home, and your belongings working for you (or against you)? Find ways to make room for simplicity.

Let It Go

Feeling overwhelmed? Simplify everything, starting with your day. Start every day with a list of seven to ten items you would like to accomplish. Now ask yourself what is essential. If you could only accomplish three tasks, which three would you choose?

Home Love Habit

As you go through the day, ask yourself if your choices and expectations for what you can fit into your home and your schedule will simplify matters or make matters more complicated. Make simplicity a habit.

4

Hardwire Habits

Wherever you are, be all there.

Jim Elliot

Do you ever wonder how anyone could possibly have everything in perfect order at all times? I mean, when you are, *ahem*, "a busy person" as most of us modern people like to refer to ourselves, you can't help but feel puzzled about how organized people have the time (or let's face it, why they care enough) to carefully fold their socks to honor them for their service, let alone unpack everything from their purse at the end of every evening so it can rest after a long day of hard work (insert blank stare and slowly blinking eyelashes).

I don't think you have to feel that you've somehow failed as a homemaker if you have ever secretly picked up a pair of your kids' socks (or your own, let's be honest) off the floor and given them a sniff to see if they could possibly be worn one more time. At least you could find matching socks, right? I think many of us feel pretty great about ourselves when we make time to care about people's feelings every day and let the socks fend for themselves. And rightfully so.

But while we may perceive the habits of organized people to be somewhat weird or annoying, perhaps we can learn a thing or two about the benefits of being a more orderly person that will inspire us.

You have probably heard that you can't (and shouldn't try to) organize clutter. To be successful, you have to declutter before you organize. But here's a little tip: You can train yourself to be more orderly before you even start to declutter, and you'll have more success. Being an orderly person will undoubtedly result in less clutter and chaos because you'll change your approach to everything. When you are intentional about your daily schedule and priorities, you can set your dominoes off in the right direction every day. Being more orderly will allow you to stop spinning your wheels and begin to focus on what is important. Creating a foundation of order in your day will bring order to all of the areas of your home.

The Habits of Organized People

We are creatures of habit, but if our daily habits aren't working for us and making our life easier and our home better, those unintentional habits will push the first domino over toward the chaotic results we experience. It might seem that productive and organized people must either have more time on their hands than the rest of us, or they must not have time for anything but organizing! But when we are organized and have productive habits, we simply don't do all the wrong things in the wrong order, causing unnecessary work and stress.

Learning how successful people function and keep their life organized can help inspire us with simple changes that will make sense for us too. I love studying how people streamline their effort and bring more order to their everyday life.

Ten Habits Organized People Incorporate into Their Day

1. They choose to be orderly to set themselves up for success. Rather than viewing organization as a chore that keeps them too busy to enjoy life, they believe that organization and less stuff allow them to enjoy life more.

2. They choose to not be emotionally attached to or hindered by stuff. When considering a purchase, they think about more than just the cost or the benefit of ownership. They also consider how that purchase could negatively impact their space or life once they own it. They quickly assess what the new item will cost them in time, upkeep, or additional clutter.

3. They say, "I'll do that now," not "I'll do that later." Organized people avoid the pileup of mess and clutter. They take care of small, everyday messes and disorder before they grow into big projects. They put their clothes directly into the hamper. Not on the bed, not on the floor, not in the bathroom...straight to the hamper! They have a place for everything and make it a habit to put things away right away. If it will only take a few minutes to do, they complete the task immediately rather than save it for later.

4. They are intentional about their mornings. They set the tone for each day by being productive right away. Simple daily tasks, such as making the bed and tidying up the bathroom (before they begin their daily work), help them to set the order for the day and inspire them to continue to be orderly, systematic, and efficient.

5. They prioritize. They create daily task lists to keep themselves focused on their goals for each day in priority order, and they focus on fully completing each task one by one. They use a large notepad or a daily calendar for their notes so they don't waste time searching for paper scraps or writing little messages in multiple locations.

They are careful not to say yes to everything that comes their way, and they feel free to say no when something will negatively impact their schedule or order of their home. They are also able to easily prioritize more time for the people and fun in their life due to the efficiency with how they complete household tasks and daily work assignments.

6. They have manageable organizational systems they can realistically maintain. Organized people do not necessarily have every shelf labeled, every closet color coded, or every drawer ready to be photographed for a magazine. Organized people know how to utilize systems that work well for them. The minute a system becomes too complicated to maintain, they find a solution that makes it more effortless and foolproof. They understand that complicated systems are just that—too complicated to maintain or remember. They have a place for everything so they can find what they need in five minutes or less.

7. They delegate. Organized people are delegators. They are effective at creating opportunities for others. They make it a priority to divide responsibility and are organized enough themselves to keep people on task and hold others accountable.

8. They cut the excuses and implement solutions. Rather than offering excuses for why something is disorganized, organized people find solutions to be more effective.

9. They keep surfaces clear. Organized people have an aversion to cluttered surfaces. They pick things up off the floor every day and clear counters regularly. They aren't necessarily minimalists in style; they simply resolve to maintain order so when clutter appears, it's recognized as something that doesn't belong and can instantly be taken care of.

10. They have systems for papers. They have a shredder and a recycling bin. They set up a location in their home and in their place of business for bills, invitations, contracts, warranties, and so on. They don't set papers all over the house or in piles on their desk and floor. When they bring the mail in, they immediately shred or recycle what they don't need. They set up a simple filing system or location for bills to pay and a place to put bills (or immediately shred them) when the bill is paid.

Does this confirm you are not an organized person? Do you fear you never will be? Trust me. It's going to be okay. Let's take this in baby steps.

Spend Mornings Intentionally

If you feel overwhelmed by where to start on reordering your priorities, not to worry! You've got this. Years ago I was desperate to figure out how to keep up with my house and everything else I was trying to do. I had a work-from-home job, two little babies to watch every day, and two middle school girls. I could not for the life of me figure out how to deal with all of the clutter and chaos of the house while keeping up with work and small people. The more cluttered and disorganized my house got, the more stressed-out mama was.

I had tried all kinds of methods, but trying to fit in a full-time effort to shape up the house was just not going to happen in that season of life. Out of desperation, I decided to try one change in how I approached housekeeping. I was going to be more intentional about how I started my day.

If you want to reorganize your home, you have to make order a priority in your day, starting with the moment you open your eyes. Mornings become like dominoes, setting the pace and tone for the entire day. Use mornings well, and everything else will slowly start to take shape.

Does the idea of establishing habits to practice in the morning send you into a bit of a panic? Think about your mornings right now. What time do you usually get up? What is the first thing you usually do? How do your mornings go? Are they stressful, or do you take a really long time to get going?

What are three things you do every morning to get the day started? Chances are you already have habits you practice every day, but they just aren't working for you because if they were effective, you would be happier with the state of your home.

If you want to have a more organized home, don't overwhelm yourself by beginning the day thinking about all the projects you could start or everything you need to do to establish order in the house. Your house didn't get disorganized overnight, right? Neither did mine! We can't expect to undo years of neglect or poor habits in one day. New habits take time.

I'm still in the process of becoming a more orderly person with a tidier house, but I think it's a fun and rewarding process, so be encouraged and enjoy the journey.

Now, don't worry if you have to head out to work or have kids who limit your time early in your day. Many of us are busy in the mornings, so you don't have to do any more than you are able to. This is about simplifying. Pick just a few habits or morning rituals you want to practice every day to set the day in motion.

Even on busy mornings, I make it a priority to at least make my bed and take care of the dishes before I settle into any other important task. Those simple tasks make me feel accomplished at the start of the day and prevent the house from spiraling out of control later. Making it a priority to make the bed and do the dishes first in the morning actually conserves energy for the rest of my priorities because I start out the day ahead and in control.

The goal is to focus on those tasks that will make the greatest impact for your day so you can move on to other things that are important to you. What tasks will make you feel more in control of your home? If you could only fit in one task before work, which one would make the biggest difference when you walk through your door in the evening? Start there. Make that one task your first daily habit.

Focus on just a few tasks every single morning until they become a routine you can't live without.

Do It Now

Design a simple morning housekeeping routine for your kids. What are three or four easy morning essentials you would like them to incorporate before school? Perhaps you list "make your bed," "hang up your towel," and "wipe out the sink before you leave." Depending on their age and if they are early risers, delegate and give them an additional housekeeping task, such as emptying the dishwasher.

Before I dive into work I look forward to a little quiet time to myself to begin the day with solitude and reflection while my husband is driving our son to school. As an introvert, I relish the rhythm of a slow, quiet start because it helps me to ease into the day in the right frame of mind.

Rushing around sets a frantic, out-of-control feeling that affects my attitude and my ability to settle into work. I'm naturally a slow starter on projects and have trouble focusing intently, so beginning the morning with a few mindless tasks and familiar rhythms gets me into the work mind-set and prepares me for what lies ahead in my day.

I feel that I have to enter a certain zone before I can really accomplish anything of significance. And boy, it's hard to get in the zone if I don't prepare myself properly to be in control from the moment I open my eyes.

What Is Your Morning Routine Like?

Take a moment to think about your typical weekday morning. What happens when you wake up? When do you get dressed? What do you do first? What are the most important things you need to accomplish in the morning? You probably already have a morning routine whether you are intentional about it or not.

How do you feel every morning? Do you wake up energized and ready to tackle the day, or do you drag through the morning dreading the next task? Are your mornings often frantic or stressful because your kitchen is buried in dirty dishes from dinner last night, so you feel anxious as you pour your morning coffee, you cannot find your shoes to get dressed, you are yelling at your kids to get in the car for school, or you are prone to running late for your first meeting of the day?

How do you feel every evening? Disorder in the morning is a domino that causes even more disorder in the evening.

While I have gained better control of my mornings and now thrive on the routine, it wasn't always that way for me. I had to learn to be an orderly person and develop morning rituals because order really didn't come naturally to me. Whether you are a morning person or not, whether you leave for work or work from home, take control of your morning routine.

Creating a this kind of routine is not rocket science, but it's amazing how little thought we give to its significance and impact on the rest of our day. When we head off on the day's adventures without thought to what we are doing, we are setting the dominoes in potentially disastrous directions. Make the decision ahead of time for how you will approach your day. Your morning routine doesn't have to take you long. In fact, I suggest it be short enough that you can easily complete it before you leave or begin work, or no later than midmorning if you don't have to rush into the day.

Don't leave decisions about how to spend your morning to your whims or to see how the day unfolds, and certainly don't let Facebook or your email decide how to spend your mornings, or you never know where you might be swept off to.

If your day usually begins with many small children trying to pry open your eyelids, you might decide to get up a half hour or hour before they tend to awaken so you can gain control of your morning before their sweet little faces even emerge from their beds. (Give yourself grace if your children are not yet sleeping through the night.)

Forgive me, because I'm sure at first getting up earlier may seem like an impossible thing to do and a horrible thing to even suggest if you are not a morning person or you already have to get up early for work. At first you will want to curse this suggestion and throw the covers back over your head as soon as your alarm goes off, but don't give in too soon. In a short time your body will adjust, and you will eventually get into the rhythm of going to sleep earlier. You may even start to look forward to your less hectic mornings, or at least reap the benefits of starting out your day quietly, deliberately, and on the right foot.

Each decision for how we will spend our morning should be made in advance so mornings become more productive. If we are being honest about how life is, we know that every morning doesn't always go like clockwork, so making the decision in advance to allow margins for the unexpected will make the rest of the day feel more effortless. If you have children, you especially are never quite sure what may be thrown at you (not literally, I hope, but figuratively). Expect the unexpected. That is why we need our early routine to be short, manageable, and doable even on a busy morning (or on those days when the dog throws up on the rug before you have even made your coffee).

My older daughter, Kylee, has her own home now and works full-time in an office. She made the decision for herself that even if she has to get up a few minutes earlier to make it happen, every morning she will unload the dishwasher and have a clean sink before she leaves for work. She knows that if she doesn't leave the house with a clean sink and empty dishwasher, she will return home at the end of the day and not want to cook dinner. She enjoys cooking, so that simple morning routine is a gift she gives herself to make room for what she loves at the end of every day.

Enjoyable Morning Rituals

I think it's important to incorporate enjoyable little rituals into your morning. What can you look forward to in the morning?

I have a coffee station all set up with my favorite mugs, a milk foamer, and a brewer so I can mindlessly but mindfully indulge in my morning coffee. I might sit for a few moments in silence, relaxing and enjoying the view outside our window.

My middle daughter, Courtney, makes her bed and straightens the couch pillows before she leaves for the day because she knows returning to an orderly space allows her to spontaneously invite friends over or even just enjoy a quiet evening at home. A less frazzled evening is worth a few extra moments at the start of the day.

Morning habits bring more clarity and peace to every day because they are decisions I don't have to wrestle over. They are tasks that have already been decided. I just have to follow through.

These simple habits start to establish a rhythm of order in a day. My morning habits, such as quiet time, making my bed, taking a shower, and getting dressed (right down to my makeup, shoes, and even earrings) become my first dominoes, setting the rest of my day in a positive direction. Each subsequent task I complete, such as unloading the dishwasher and polishing up the sink, reminds me that I am on the right course for the day, so I waste less of the morning feeling indecisive about what to do next or inadvertently making a less productive choice.

As I mastered morning routines, order throughout the day started feeling more natural to me. Once my bed was made consistently, I was always dressed for the day, and my kitchen was kept clean, I was inspired and more energized for accomplishing other things I'd previously felt I didn't have time for.

Soon I seemed to have more time for tackling the decluttering and organizing projects I had put off for years, as well as for embracing simple pleasures, such as creativity in the house and puttering around the garden. A morning routine is an essential domino to set up to have room for everything else in our day.

If you are struggling with starting a morning routine, simplify it. Maybe you are trying to tackle too much at once or are too overwhelmed by the possibilities and all the needs in front of you. Even if you just start with insisting that you make your bed before you head out on the day and polishing your bathroom sink—just those two tasks—you'll benefit from the consistency.

Give yourself a month to get in the rhythm, and don't let yourself skip a day with your morning routines. Something as simple as *deciding* to make the bed or to keep your sink clear every day may seem insignificant in the grand scheme of all the clutter you face in your home, but in time these simple decisions will be transformative to establishing order in other ways.

Develop Daily Habits

It won't be long before you practice your morning habits like a pro and you'll start to see a little more order in the house. High fives!

The Dailies

Keeping up our house and making room for what we love begins with committing to keep up with basic daily tasks. Here are the dailies I focus on:

1. Diligence with dishes.

2. Little bit of laundry love.

3. Bring the bed back to beautiful.

4. Cleaning frenzies. Pick a different room or surface every day to care for at least 15 minutes (declutter, tidy, and polish up). On the weekend or during a dedicated block of time, do a complete declutter of a space or clean a room top to bottom!

Getting my morning routine down was the most life-changing step for me in transforming the function of my home. It was also the first time I had a sense of myself as someone who was (somewhat) in control of her home. Even my husband noticed the changes in our home and even in me simply because of how intentional I became with decisions about my mornings.

Once you have your own mornings down pat, you'll probably find it a piece of cake to be intentional throughout the day. Morning routines are the dominoes that start to inspire other daily habits, so I have a sneaky feeling you'll find you are already incorporating a few new habits later in the day as a result. If not, don't worry. We can add one habit at a time!

What are some daily habits you should incorporate as an intentional part of every day? I find it helpful to break my day into multiple little routines that help me keep up with the biggest mess producers in our home, namely dishes and the laundry. The key is being decisive about the fact that you will stick to these biggest offenders every day and not put off any essential tasks. The effect of putting off these tasks will compound the problem and add to the clutter and general disarray of your home. Be decisive about what you are going to do every day and follow through on your decisions.

Personally, I didn't have much success with assigning different tasks to different days of the week or every other day because that seemed to involve too much thinking and too many choices (I would have to actually remember what day it was, I didn't want to spend time deliberating which days were best to do what, and I definitely didn't want to expend all that energy to keep up with that detailed of a schedule).

Dishes

While you may thrive on assigning tasks to each day of the week, some tasks cannot be left to just once a week without causing more calamities. Putting off dishes until Tuesday, for instance, will be a disaster unless you never eat at home. To simplify everything else you need to do, dishes should be washed every day, followed by wiping up the counters and sink without fail.

Yes, that can feel like a full-time job if you aren't used to doing dishes every day. But imagine how much work and stress you create when you save them all for the weekend? When you save dishes for another day, every day your kitchen becomes a little bit messier, a little bit more difficult to clean, and a lot more likely to attract more clutter and mess. Not to mention you'll feel worse and worse about the state of your home as the week goes on, making you more likely to fall into despair and leave other tasks undone. At least that is what happens at my house! I need clear expectations for myself when it comes to domino habits like doing my dishes.

Fortunately, if you keep up on dishes every day, it becomes more of an autopilot task. It's a nonnegotiable decision that has already been made for your day. You can skip a lot of other housekeeping tasks and your home won't be all that be adversely affected, but dishes shouldn't be negotiated.

Laundry

Speaking of tasks we can't put off without the entire household falling apart, we are all too familiar with the task of laundry, so we might as well make the process as streamlined and pleasant as possible. Because it's a never-ending chore, I make it a habit to keep up with it every day. Now, don't start panicking, thinking you can't possibly do laundry every day along with dishes, either because you don't have that much laundry (lucky you) or because you'd rather not do dishes and laundry on the same day (understandable). This is the plan that works for me to keep order in my home, because just like with dishes, when laundry piles up, it becomes almost insurmountable.

If, for instance, I have the freedom to put laundry off until Saturday and then decide that is the first day of the weekend so I would rather go hang gliding than do laundry (not that I would decide that with my extreme fear of heights, but just if I did), by the following Thursday no one would have undies (setting off a search throughout the house in hopes no one had put the clean laundry away the previous week). By Friday people are upset that they can't find their favorite jeans (likely to result in shopping if said jeans are not located in time), but, of course, by this point no one can get into the laundry room because the pile is blocking the door. To attempt to break into the laundry room would result in various injuries, so laundry is then avoided for another week.

Does this fiasco sound like a woman who should be trusted to do laundry on whatever schedule or day suits her fancy? I rest my case.

I cannot possibly give myself the freedom of a decision as weighty as whether or not I should do laundry on a Tuesday or a Thursday (because, naturally, if given the choice, I will choose to put it off if there is any freedom at all to negotiate on days). I do laundry every day to simplify, to keep my daily rhythm consistent, and to avoid any wasted energy or resulting calamity due to indecision.

To further keep things tidy around the house, I (or whoever the task is delegated to—delegate whenever possible) need to complete the entire task: wash, dry, fold or hang, and put away. I don't believe in adding extra steps, such as piling clothes first on the sofa, then putting the clothes in laundry baskets where they sit for a day or two before finally making it to the appropriate room, or tossing them on the floor to fold later and then having to rewash because they have been on the floor all week. It helps to plan laundry around times we are home so we can set timers to take things out of the dryer and immediately hang or put away to avoid wrinkles and ironing.

Love It

Treat yourself to a more inviting laundry space so you'll be more inspired to keep up with the task! Polish up the washer and dryer and toss out lint. Remove old detergent containers and put detergent in prettier containers or at least clean them up and set them up in a more attractive way. If you have room, hang a revolving gallery of pretty prints or homemade art using clothespins. Use the back of the door to hang a pocket shoe organizer for supplies. Set up a basket system for dirty clothes, cleaning rags, and wayward socks.

Let's say I literally don't have clothing to wash today. Yay, me! I'm caught up on clothes. But I'm not off the hook. Every day is laundry day, so I will wash blankets or rugs or sheets. Maybe I'll wash the shower curtains or do some delicate hand washing that otherwise would be easy to put off forever. Even when I don't have enough laundry to justify a load or the time to do actual laundry, I still find it helps to do some sort of laundry-based activity every day just to stay on course. Maybe I'll even iron tablecloths and napkins (just kidding). I probably wouldn't choose to iron, but I can always wipe down the tops of the washer and dryer, or mop the laundry room floor, or even just tidy up the detergent. Honestly, if I skip a day here and there? Not the end of the world because laundry has become such a habit that I can get myself right back in the rhythm knowing how much better it is to stay on task.

If you like to break down a task into a more specific daily laundry schedule to post in your laundry room or add to your home notebook, break down your laundry like this or modify it as needed:

Monday—Towels and whites

Tuesday—Darks and jeans

Wednesday—Delicates, shower curtains, and bath rugs

Thursday—Family's sheets

Friday—Master bedroom sheets and towels

If I can keep up with dishes and laundry every day, I feel as if I can conquer anything. Give it a try!

Defeat Clutter

Every home has clutter magnets—or hot spots, as they are often called. Can you find yours? Perhaps your kitchen counter is a clutter magnet. Dishes, papers, lunch boxes, mail, tweezers...it all ends up there. What about your nightstand? Your coffee table? Your floor? Any surface is at risk.

Where does most of your daily clutter land and the frustration begin? Let's not mess around here. Clutter wants to take over your home and make you feel defeated. It wants you to think your house is a complete wreck and you are powerless to conquer it because every day it's there, taunting you. You might tackle a surface one day, and the next day you head back in the room and all you can hear is "WE'RE BAAAACK!" So not nice. It's a lie from the pit, but we believe it because when we look around, we are understandably overwhelmed. It just won't go away.

Sometimes you need a quick fix with a long-term solution that gives you hope that you've got this thing. I'm right there with you. If you can identify your key clutter landing spots and defeat those surfaces once and for all, your home will look instantly better, even if the rest of your house still needs help. Are you with me?

Do It Now

What are some habits you could set up for your main living space? Let the whole family be involved in keeping things tidy there. Perhaps always do a quick cleaning frenzy before everyone heads to bed or leaves the room. TV remotes go back in the basket. Dishes are taken to the kitchen. Paper is recycled. Game controls have to be put back into their bins. Make it a goal to not let mess pile up!

An entire house to declutter and organize can feel overwhelming, but in order to not pass out when you look around and think about all that needs to be done, let's just think about the key visible areas around the home. Think in terms of surfaces that attract daily mess. Now, I'm not saying that just dealing with the clutter magnets is going to solve all your clutter problems. It won't. But I can tell you, without a doubt, for sure, that if you can defeat clutter in a few areas and ban those spots from ever getting out of control again, you'll feel a whole bunch better about your home, and you'll develop new habits too. And when you feel better, you'll be inspired to tackle more. Defeating hot spots is like a miracle worker when we are about to give up. So let's do this!

I like to break down projects into smaller, more manageable tasks, so I suggest you start with just two to three areas that REALLY drive you crazy every day. You can pick just one if you want, but if you are an overachiever, you'll feel more accomplished if you do a few at once. And, honestly, it's not that hard to do several because we are talking LITTLE areas, not big ones. Focus on what would be manageable surfaces or small sections of rooms rather than entire rooms.

Perhaps areas such as:

- your kitchen or bathroom counters
- the dining table
- the floor around the front door or around your closet
- the laundry room floor
- your nightstand

If you have more than a few areas that need an overhaul, don't stress out. You can get to those later. If you have one room that is a real problem every day, perhaps pick just two manageable surfaces near each other, such as the closet floors and dresser top in that one space. In fact, if you have two dressers in a room, you might put both surfaces on your hit list because you don't want to just divert clutter from one spot to the next!

Don't you feel better already knowing you don't have to attack the clutter in the whole house?

You can do this. I promise. A clean surface will become a domino habit. It's amazing what clear surfaces will do for your state of mind and your motivation to keep it that way.

Grab a box and spend a little bit of time clearing each of your clutter hot spots, dumping everything into the box. It's not going to stay in the box and end up in the garage, and we aren't going to start with buying bins or containers to "organize" everything into a new container.

Right now we are just clearing the surfaces into the box so you can see that spot for how it should be, a peaceful rest for your eyes rather than a resting place for clutter. Now step back and look at that pretty and clear surface! Ahhh. So much better.

Obviously, you are going to end up with piles of stuff in a box that used to be in the hot spot and are now without a home. Good. That surface was not their home. Nor is the box their new home, so don't let them get too comfortable in it. Empty the contents of the box and take each item to its proper home. If something doesn't have a home, create one on a shelf, in a container, on a hook, or send it packing. You'll be working more on decluttering and organizing your home as you go, so don't overthink this step and worry too much, and definitely don't get sidetracked organizing other areas of the home.

> *The goal of decluttering your clutter magnets is simply to change the purpose of the hot spot from a former clutter magnet to a peaceful oasis in that space.*

Now your job is to protect those clear surfaces with your life. You will have to defend it from clutter that wants to take up residence there. Go all full gazelle when you see clutter try to creep back. You might find yourself shouting (in your head), "STEP AWAY FROM THAT SUR-FACE!" when you find yourself unexpectedly setting something there. Or if you enter the room, and lo and behold an unnamed intruder has deposited items there in a sneak attack, *deal with it right then, or at least by the end of the day before you head to bed*. It only takes a few moments if you keep up on it.

I'll admit that at our house we occasionally have to put little signs in certain areas to be a reminder that we aren't going to put clutter here. Try a sign that says "Clutter, this is not your home" if you want to be gentle but firm with the people and clutter that gravitate there.

Adopting daily habits and keeping hot spots clear will not mean your home will magically declutter overnight, but I promise you that being intentional about your day will change your habits, and before you know it, your home will start to become more orderly with less effort.

Pause, Reflect, and Act

Make Room

Habits are friends, not foes. Have you resisted habits because you want to be free and spontaneous? When we become more intentional with what we do during the day and how we use our time, we have *more* room for spontaneity and creativity. What do we really want to do in life? How could being more efficient with our daily tasks make more room for things that are truly important to us?

Let It Go

Grab a pen and make two columns on a piece of paper or in a notebook. On one side, make a list of words that describe the current state of your mornings. List the default habits, such as perhaps mindlessly surfing your phone or oversleeping. On the right side of the column, make a list of what your true priorities should be and how you want to spend your mornings. Write out three new goals for your mornings. How will you feel if you stick to your new goals?

Home Love Habit

Get in the habit of order in your home. Which clutter hot spots will you start with? Make a short list of one to three of the worst offenders and commit to keeping those areas clear. Post the list on your mirror and keep tabs on them daily. Soon you'll find it's a habit to keep surfaces clutter-free!

5

Evict Excuses

If you can't fly, then run.
If you can't run, then walk.
If you can't walk, then crawl.
But whatever you do,
you have to keep moving forward.

MARTIN LUTHER KING JR.

I know what you are probably thinking about now. *This domino habit concept and creating a peaceful oasis business sounds nice in theory, but you don't know my kids.*

You are thinking I haven't seen the mess your kids make. You are thinking your kids are the ones who set the dominoes in motion, and they know just what to topple over so the whole house falls apart! If it were only up to you, your home would be in perfect order. Or you might be shaking your head, saying under your breath, "You don't know my husband. He doesn't do dishes." "You don't understand my situation. I work outside the home." "My house is too small." "My house is too big."

Many people have ongoing excuses for why their home is so out of control, even justifying clutter in a positive light by explaining that they are a fun person or a spontaneous friend and just don't have time for the house. Who can argue with that? Perhaps you have priorities, and being organized isn't one of them. That makes sense...except it doesn't, really.

The truth is, structuring our home around a reasonable amount of order rather than chaos will give us more time, not less, for all of those things we need or want to do. And when our house is more organized, we'll be happier doing everything we want to do. To take back control of your house, you'll need to get on board to own this mission and evict the excuses you've been hiding behind.

Take Responsibility

Your home should be your sanctuary, don't you agree? I totally get that there are real reasons why we struggle with clutter in spite of what we want our home to be like. But if you want to change your home, something has to change in how you deal with it. As the heart and keeper of your home, you have the power to transform where you live. Excuses to the contrary are just that, justifying the reasons why we won't do something. You might have great excuses why this will be challenging for you, but everything worth having is worth pursuing.

My husband and I don't watch a lot of TV together, but we really got into the TV series *Parenthood* because it was one we could both enjoy. We were late bloomers when it came to that show, but we watched the entire series back-to-back over a few months on Netflix after the show had already ended for the rest of the world. *Parenthood* is about a family and all the ups and downs they go through together.

There was one episode where Grandpa was in counseling with Grandma because he wasn't being sensitive to her needs. The counselor gave him a tip. He was supposed to show he was understanding by saying, "I hear you and I see you" whenever Grandma poured out her heart to him. My husband and I laughed so hard at him saying, "I hear you and I see you," but isn't that what we all really want? We want other people to acknowledge how we feel. We want people to understand our pain, our challenges, our misery, our feelings. We don't want to feel alone or go through challenges without our people on board.

Well, I don't know if this will help you in this situation or not, but I hear you. I do. I see you there overwhelmed by clutter so high you can't even remember what is at the bottom of the pile. I see you there, Mama, pointing to the mess your four (adorable, by the way!) kids age five and under made of the living room while you simply tried to take a two-minute shower alone. I see you there in that teeny, tiny house with no closets. I see you there doing your best on your own, working all day long. I hear you, friend, discouraged by the challenging situation you have to face every day. I see you trying to explain to your man and offspring the wonderful features in your home, such as laundry hampers and dishwashers. I do. I see you.

You may even struggle in other ways, physically or emotionally, and my heart feels for you. You may not be able to take all of the suggestions I offer—and that's okay. Don't put undue pressure on yourself if you are already dealing with more than you can handle. Just do what you can, improve where you can, and let go of the rest.

We are in this together even from afar, you and me, but if we are going to transform our home and make room for what we love, we will have to own our own mission. I'm here to be your cheerleader, but I can't own your mission for you. And you can't own it yourself if you blame everyone else for how you ended up in the mess you are in. You might not be the only one responsible for making the mess, but you will likely care more than anyone else about finding the way out of it. That's why you need to lead the way.

As much as you might prefer to be a DIY kind of girl, there are times when you simply can't do it yourself. Try bartering or doing a project swap with a friend or neighbor, reach out to a local church that may have a servant team (if you called our church and you lived in our community, we'd be pumped to help you, so don't hesitate to reach out to people who want to serve), or if you can afford some help, hire someone to assist you! Whatever you do, don't just sit there wallowing in despair. Getting a house in order is more fun when you are not doing it alone.

If your home is really out of control, you may feel as if you have far too many obstacles in the way of getting things done. I'm sure you will face days and challenges that might make this whole process seem impossible at times. You'll want to give up. You might feel like you already have to do everything else by yourself, so why do you have to figure this out too? Here's a reason to think about: Because you deserve this. That's why. You deserve to have a home that inspires you, not be stuck living in one that makes you want to cry.

That's not to say you shouldn't expect your family to do their part. They just might not have the same passion for it that you do. Even if you are the only gazelle in the house passionate enough to get things rolling, you can change everything (and even inspire the rest of the family) if you put your heart and soul into this.

Get Organized as a Family

Sometimes I felt that a shining accomplishment on any day when my kids were growing up was getting everyone out the door with pants on. Trying to keep up with the laundry, the dishes, the toys, the big kids' schedule, the little kids' tantrums, the job; taking care of the house-work, the cooking, the grocery shopping, the bills, the closets, the clut-ter, the dog; avoiding stepping on Legos; and getting to preschool on time? That's a lot to ask. Add the crazy requirement that everyone must have pants on, and I pretty much lost the will to leave the house.

When my son was just a toddler, he was on the sofa one afternoon next to my nephew, both of them sitting side by side with their little legs straight out and happily playing with toy tools lined up around them. I was in the kitchen nearby when suddenly I hear one of those things you never expect to hear from your own flesh and blood (even if it was in a sweet, little-boy, singsongy voice): "I've got a hammmmer and it's going to be oouuuuchy!" I've never turned my head to see what was happening so fast in my entire life.

Now, in his defense it was just a plastic toy, and he wasn't even swinging at his cousin (thankfully). But after a little mom-to-son pep talk about being a little more sensitive in the future to avoid scaring people with threats of injury by hammers, I went in the other room and laughed until tears were rolling down my face. I can't help but chuckle about that story even now, but I haven't fully trusted my son with a hammer ever since.

Tell me I'm not alone on this. Being a mom is like running a three-ring circus. Just trying to keep everyone jumping through the right hoops (let alone keeping everyone dressed) seems almost like an insurmountable feat sometimes. If we can't keep up with it all already, how in the world can we keep their rooms organized or even get them to help us do it?

You have a lot on your plate already, mama; you don't need anything extra to complicate your life. Here is one simple trick you can try that will bring a little more sanity into your kids' toy space and create a lot less work for you. Are you ready for it?

Give them less stuff.

"It's so much fun reorganizing the playroom every day when the kids dump out all 30 color-sorted, organized cubbies of small toys, crafts, and tiny game pieces into a giant heap on the playroom floor!" *said no mom in the history of ever.*

I know we love the idea of giving kids many options of what to play with, and we have dreams of getting all those neat little cubbies for every possible craft and perfectly organized bins so they can select from hundreds of accessories for Polly Pocket's various fashionable accessories sorted by summer, winter, and fall essentials, but who really has time to keep up with all that?

If you can't keep up with their things and they don't keep up with them, it's like wondering why your head hurts even as you are banging it against the wall. You aren't a mean mom if you limit how much stuff they have to make a mess of. You are a good mom for teaching them to value what they have and appreciate it.

Less stuff might sound like less fun for the kids, but in reality they will appreciate each toy more and maybe even be inspired to get a little more creative when they aren't overwhelmed and distracted by excessive options. You can always rotate toys in so they can still enjoy a variety of fun things, just not all at the same time.

Teaching kids the value of simplicity and being content with less when they are young will impact them in healthy ways for a lifetime, so look for ways to pare down excess and streamline what they have to deal with.

Give them less to put away and less to clean up, and model the value of spending time together enjoying experiences over managing stuff. Try the same for the whole family, and see how your family dynamics change.

Do It Now

If you have young kids, take a look at their toys. Do they have so many within reach that they can't possibly keep them organized? Pare them down to only a few things your children can play with without your help and put the rest out of reach for times when you can better supervise.

When my kids were younger, we put only limited or even no toys or craft supplies in their bedroom. Separating out most of their toys and crafts to other spaces in the house gave the kids a sense that bedrooms are for sleeping, reading, and quiet play, not for the wild rumpus that would ensue when there were dozens of options to distract them.

Having fewer toys and craft supplies in their room also served to teach the kids to value their space by making it less complicated to take care of. I really wanted my kids to take ownership of their own room, so they got to choose how to personalize it. I gave them a variety of designs and color choices and encouraged their involvement in decorating and setting up their space. With a bit less stuff in the room to fuss over, and more connection to their own room, they more effortlessly tidied their bookshelves, pick up their stuffed animals, and put away their clothes.

To organize their spaces, divide their room into functional zones for sleeping, reading books, and dressing, and set up each one with what they need. Create a separate zone (in another room or designated spot within their bedroom) for toys, and another one for table-type work, such as homework or crafts.

Toys and crafts should be as simply organized by category as possible. Give them buckets or bins to store things. Add labels for each that are specific enough to make sense (dolls, Barbie's clothes, blocks, costumes, balls, tools) but not so detailed (Polly Pocket's blue tank tops,

Barbie's long party dresses) that the process of organization and clean-up becomes a tedious nightmare and a source of frustration. Save your own sanity by keeping bins with toys that involve tiny pieces up high and out of reach, and only bring them down when you can supervise.

Help kids to become orderly people. Give them their own shelves to store special things they like, inspiration boards to be creative, and let them help create labels for bins and make suggestions on how to organize. Show them how much space is available for toys or craft supplies, and tell them they can only keep what fits in there. They can decide what to let go of based on how much room they have available.

Kids thrive on routine the way adults do, so dole out the daily habits to everyone in the house! Give everyone their own morning routine and a household task suitable for their age and current needs. Even toddlers can learn to help make their beds, dust, and bring laundry to the hamper. Young kids can help feed pets, set tables, fold laundry, and help with matching socks.

Each child can help take care of their own room and pitch in to care for the bathrooms and public areas of the house. Set everyone up for success by giving them clear direction about where to put their own belongings every day, and walk them through the routine steps for what to do when they leave the house in the morning and return home at night. Of course, don't make their daily routines too difficult. Simple done well is better than complicated but never practiced.

10 Ways to Organize the Family for a New School Year

1. Simplify the morning chaos. Take a look at your entry. Does every child have a designated spot for their schoolbag, sports equipment, and coat? If you don't have space in the entry, look around for a convenient location. You might decide to create a landing zone in the child's bedroom or closet for their belongings. Having designated places for everything they need will cut down on the entry overflow and morning chaos.

2. Manage the family schedule. Where are you going to keep those sport schedules and school calendars? You can use a cell phone or computer calendar if you prefer an electronic version, or you can find a visible place to post or file all the papers and calendars your children will bring home from school the first week. Find a wall to put up a large family calendar or bulletin board and establish a system for organizing schedules, holding papers, and displaying important reminders.

3. Create designated workspaces. Where will your kids do homework after school? Take some time to clean up a home office, bedroom desk, or set up a kids' homework table in the family room. Start with a clear surface. Throw away any old, worn-out pens and pencils and replace them with fresh ones. Stock drawers or baskets with fresh notebook paper, printer ink, and any other school supplies.

4. Organize the fridge. Prepare for mealtimes and give the refrigerator a deep cleaning. Put a plastic bin or basket in the fridge to corral healthy snack and lunch items to make packing a lunch easy. Hang a chalkboard or magnetic notepad on the fridge with a list of weekly breakfast, lunch, and snack ideas so kids can help prepare their own meals.

5. Tidy the pantry. Get the pantry ready for packing lunches and quick breakfasts. Clear out some pantry space or a cabinet drawer for supplies. Stock up on lunch bags, sandwich baggies, snack containers, napkins, and a water bottle for each child.

6. Clear the clutter. It always feels great to have less clutter in the house. Grab a trash bag (or a few) and go through the house filling up bags with any unnecessary clutter. Donate, give to friends, recycle, or throw away. You will breathe a sigh of relief the more you remove! Concentrate on bedrooms, kitchen, and family spaces first so those areas are clutter-free and ready for the season.

7. Set up kids' bedrooms. Kids will feel more organized and able to get themselves ready for school if their rooms are cleared out and their belongings are streamlined. Every year kids outgrow toys and end up with supplies and books from previous school years. Let the kids be involved in eliminating what is no longer needed. Clear their nightstands and start fresh with only a few key items, such as a clock, a lamp, and a few favorite books. Help them feel organized and ready for a new year with under-the-bed storage, new baskets, an organized dresser, etc.

8. *Pare down clothes.* If your kids have outgrown all their school clothes, it's time to clear out the old. No use leaving too-small clothing items in the closet or they might end up wearing them or being frustrated trying to find things that fit. Go through everything now and give away good clothes that no longer fit to shelters or donation centers. Go through sock and underwear drawers to make sure everything is stocked with clean items that still fit.

9. *Refresh the bathroom.* Deep clean the bathroom! Clean under sinks and in drawers. Make sure each child has what they need to get ready in the morning so they will be more eager to get dressed without your prodding. Hang a morning schedule on the mirror so younger kids can remember basic expectations on school mornings, such as getting dressed and brushing teeth and hair.

10. *Corral homework, backpacks, and sport bags.* Last but not least, it's time to rally the school supplies and pack those backpacks. The annual tradition of a new or cleaned-out backpack makes a great transition for kids to a more scheduled and organized fall. Let your kids clean out their old backpack, or if you are starting fresh, let them help pick out their new one. Get them involved in labeling everything and deciding how to organize their own school supplies and backpacks. Show kids their designated landing zone and where you will want them to put things after school. Talk to them about their school morning routines and show them their homework area. Letting kids be involved in the why and how of organizing will help them to be more successful in school and will cut down on frustrations at home.

Make Room for Sanity in Small Spaces

I've lived in big houses and little houses, and while big houses sometimes get a bad rap for having a lot of surfaces to clean, they feel much easier to tidy up because clutter is barely noticeable. And let's face it, a big house has plenty of room to acquire lots and lots of things without realizing what you are doing. Small houses are my favorite, but they require a special type of attention to keep them organized and free of excess. With limited space to stash things, we have to be intentional about using well the space we have and refuse to let clutter fill every nook and cranny.

A small room can be just as functional, attractive, and comfortable as a larger one if you know the secrets to maximizing your space. As always, start by decluttering down to what is essential and what really brings you joy. Be ruthless in a small space to only keep what is truly practical and useful, but don't fear that decluttering in a small house means you can't enjoy the things you love.

Five Ideas to Make the Most Room in a Small Space

1. Go vertical. Make the most of vertical space and get things off the floors. Tall and narrow bookshelves are the perfect solution to hold items in a room with limited floor space. Look for one that's extra tall and fill it up with pretty books, accessories, and storage boxes.

2. Secret storage. In a tiny living room, a round storage ottoman will allow for an easy, flowing traffic pattern in and out of the conversation area as well as the extra space you need to stash your remotes or other necessities.

3. Little carts. Not enough storage in your small kitchen? Try tucking in a rolling cart with drop leaf sides against a wall or in a corner in or near your kitchen. A little cart can be an extra work surface when you need it and additional storage space. Add hooks and a towel bar for small accessories or oven mitts. For extra convenience and flexibility, add casters so it can be rolled in and out of the kitchen as needed.

4. Corner pieces. In a small space, every corner counts. If you need a little extra space for your favorite dishes or serving pieces, put a small corner to use! Corner cabinets can be especially useful in a dining room or kitchen or even in the corner of a small bathroom or bedroom.

5. Dual function. You can maximize a small space efficiently by utilizing furnishings that serve multiple functions. Stools can serve as an extra seat but also as a side table for cups and plates, or as a perch for reading material next to a chair or sofa.

Do It Now

Take control of an area of your home. Look at your nightstand. What's on it? Dust the surface and only put back what you actually need—perhaps a lamp, a clock or a charger for your cell phone, and a stack of a few favorite books topped with a candle in a glass jar or on a small saucer.

Go on Therapeutic Frenzies

One thing you might notice as you go through the house on any given day is a lot of what I call unnecessary clutter. Clutter should never be "necessary," but in this case I'm talking about the things people have just set down and moved on without putting them where they belong. Little piles scattered about the house. Yes, ideally we won't have clutter at all if everyone in the household is doing their job and putting their belongings away, but let's be honest. Clutter will sometimes still happen.

We might walk around and see a clothes hanger left on a coffee table, a dirty sock on the dining table (why?), coats on the bathroom floor. I don't know about you, but sometimes the random things that seem to appear out of nowhere amuse me. One day I found a bookmark my daughter made in third grade on our kitchen counter. My daughter had already graduated from college. How did it end up on the counter? I just left it sitting there, thinking I would put it away later. Soon other bits and random things joined it. There was a large screw, a tiny llama key chain with no keys attached to it, a hair tie, a cord to something, several Post-it Notes, and a granola bar wrapper. At this point there was a collection of miscellaneous things, so in an effort to tidy up, I tossed it all in a bowl (I threw away the wrapper, however). The bowl now traveled from room to room, picking up more clutter and always filled with things no one claimed.

If we choose to leave even one random bit lying about, chances are it will grow and multiply. We need to make an intentional commitment to prevent the multiplication of disorder. We want to create forward motion toward order, so we need to nip these little bits of randomness while they are just forming. Even though it is frustrating sometimes, I'm committed to tidying up as I go through the day to prevent messes from multiplying (teach your family to do the same), always taking even small opportunities to make a space a little better than when I found it.

Every day I run around the house in a quick frenzy to clean up any potential clutter. Yes, I could be annoyed that I have clutter and refuse to deal with it because I didn't make the mess. Yes, I can get annoyed that my family still leaves things sitting out. Yes, I even get mad at myself that we still have piles. But the fact of the matter is, clutter exists, and no matter whose fault it is, I choose to go on these little tidying frenzies as therapeutic rituals for me and for my house.

And you know what? If I keep up on it, usually the room is not quite as out of control as it initially appears. In a smallish house, a few misplaced things look like out-of-control chaos, but once I dive in, I may find it only took five minutes to put it all back where it belonged. The results of my few moments of frenzy are simple: My house is tidier and I'm happier. Sometimes we make resetting our home a more difficult process than it needs to be because we become fixated on the fact that other people should not put stuff in random places, and that paralyzes us from being in control of our own sanity.

In time, your new gazelle focus on tidiness will likely rub off on everyone else—or at least perhaps inspire them so you can subtly train your people. Meanwhile, don't let anyone, or anything, steal your serenity (or your sanity). This home is your sanctuary.

Love It

Start a new weekly ritual of clearing clutter and restoring order in one area of your house. Each week pick a different area to attack. Set aside a block of time on your calendar and don't let anything crowd it out! First, get inspired. Find photos for how you dream your space will look once it is clean. Post your favorite image in the room the week before and start dreaming of tidiness! Play some energizing tunes, put on a cleaning outfit (I like to wear lace-up, comfy boots, jeans, and a T-shirt or sweatshirt), and make decluttering and tidying your house a celebratory event.

The truth is, creating the environment I want and doing it quietly without a major rant probably takes less energy than I would have expended had I started fussing about everyone else's lack of motivation or ignored it all in protest until it became a giant ordeal.

If you feel overwhelmed with how much there is to do in any given space, set aside just a few moments to tackle something and ask yourself this one question that will help you zero in on a doable action: "What is one thing I could do in the next five minutes in this space that would make the biggest impact?"

Be more intentional with how you invest the time you have available. It's amazing what you can do in pockets of time. You probably have a spare few minutes here and there, right? Whenever you have a moment and see a little job to do, take advantage of it. Moments add up to progress.

Five Ways to Get Better Organized with a Little Therapeutic Frenzy

1. Straighten up your coffee table. Corral objects and remotes in a drawer or a tray.

2. Declutter the desk. Recycle paper and shred unneeded documents. Put pens in a cup. Dust the tabletop.

3. Tidy your bathroom. Dump out the trash, take things off the counter and put everything back where it belongs, wipe off the counters, swish the toilet bowl with a handy-dandy cleaning wand, and sweep the floors.

4. Wipe off the kitchen counters. Sticky spots and crumbs on the counter can be wiped up in a matter of minutes.

5. Clear the floor. Look around your entry. Is the floor cluttered with things to return, backpacks, and briefcases? Take a few moments to clear the floor as you pass through.

When I have a spare five minutes, instead of just sitting down in my chair staring at Facebook to avoid thinking about what to do next, I have learned to use that small opportunity to look for a domino I can topple over.

Harnessing Little Pockets of Time

1. *While you get ready for the day.* As you are putting on your makeup in the morning, take a few moments to notice what products you automatically reach for. Now see what else is in your makeup bag or drawer. If there are products you use only on occasion, put those in a separate container away from your everyday items. If you find you never end up opening that container, let those items go to make more room for what you really love.

2. *While you are getting dressed.* What are three things you could remove from your closet that make you feel frumpy every time you put them on? If you find yourself hesitating on what to choose, ask yourself if you would buy the item again right now if you didn't already own it. If the answer is no, you should let it go. Give items away to someone who will feel beautiful in them and free more breathing room in your closet at the same time. Take those items with you when you head out for the day.

3. *While you are getting ready for bed.* Make it a nightly ritual to quickly tidy a clutter magnet in your bedroom (it may be your bedside table, dresser top, or the floor) before your head hits the pillow. You'll thank yourself in the morning when you wake up to one less mess.

Pause, Reflect, and Act

Make Room

What are your goals for your home? How have excuses kept you from achieving them? Success in your home and life starts with a mind-set. What do you really want to make more room for? Use SMART goals to make that happen!

Let It Go

What are some cluttered areas that have stayed that way for months because you've found excuses to not deal with them? Don't let excuses rob you of your joy. How could you get past the excuses and start making more progress?

Home Love Habit

What new, daily habit could you incorporate to achieve your goals of a tidier house? Journal in your notebook about how an excuse has been keeping you from your goals. Write the new habit down in your home notebook or journal.

6

Be Focused

You can do anything, but not everything.

DAVID ALLEN

You might be wondering how you could possibly find time for anything more in your day when you already have so much to do. Are you pulled ragged in every direction, or always running around like a chicken with its head cut off? Certainly, I must be able to share a secret to multitasking effectively so you will be able to get all the daily tasks done and still find time for what you really love to do, right?

How we spend our day changes everything about how our home functions and feels, and the daily decisions we commit to will direct us toward, or away from, our goals.

Who has time for keeping a house tidy when you are juggling so many other responsibilities all day?

And if you are a mom of little ones, you probably feel as if you have miniature tornadoes blowing through the living room every day. Is it really possible with kids to have a productive schedule for housekeeping, let alone time to even think about other life goals? You may spend a good chunk of every day keeping one eye on your daredevil toddler, who might decide unexpectedly to skydive off the second floor balcony, and the other eye on your baby, who would love nothing more than to experiment with smashing bananas on your couch cushions between feedings and getting her diaper changed.

On top of it all, like many women, you might juggle work in or out of the home. At the end of every day, you...are...wiped...out. Who has energy to do more?

As far as I know, no one has ever found more hours in a day. We all have just 24 to work with.

You envision a goal of a tidy house, but your most important priorities are probably never more obvious than when you have tiny faces looking up at you.

Housekeeping shouldn't consume all of your energy or keep you from what matters, but lack of order in the house will eventually drain what little reserves you do have. Fortunately, we don't have to live with regret or be distracted from what is really important to us.

It's those tiny faces, or those big dreams you have, or those grand callings in life that should be a reminder of exactly *why* this mission of decluttering and organizing your home *matters*. You do have more important things to do with your life than housekeeping, so let's make a plan to put more energy into those priorities and not waste so much of it managing *stuff* we don't need anymore. No, I'm not saying to stop cleaning your house to go chase your dreams! I'm saying let's get a handle on what needs to be done and when to do it, and be ruthless about what we really need and don't need in our life so our attention isn't diffused in many directions.

How can we best manage our day to make more room in it for everything that matters to us? The real secret to success is to learn how to harness your energy so you can focus it effectively on the present task at hand and on your priorities throughout the day and week.

Use Your Energy Well

If you are trying to juggle it all, including wonderful aspirations and goals such as motherhood, business, volunteering, college, a calling, a job, or dream chasing, can you ever achieve that elusive balance you strive for in what you want to accomplish, alongside of your quest for contentment right where you are?

I've wrestled with those issues too.

Even after years of running my blog, *The Inspired Room*, from my home, and many years prior to that working from home while raising my kids, managing time was challenging. While I really had tried through the years to balance my work and housework with chore charts or checking off to-do lists, I struggled with the same problems you probably do when there is literally too much to do. It was hard to figure out how to keep up when it felt that I simply did not have enough time.

In my search for a better way to manage everything on my plate, including my home, I experimented with a lot of ways to bring more order to my life. I read books on time management. I particularly gleaned insight and wisdom from business-related books, such as *The One Thing* and *Essentialism*, that I have applied to how I can best manage my home as well. I've incorporated what works and found things that inspired me with how to better manage my energy reserves on the tasks in front of me every day.

It makes sense to me that a better-managed life in *general* impacts every part of my day, my home, and my priorities. While I don't have it all together, I do find it helpful to consider how to balance my energy throughout the day and my life as a whole rather than worry about how much time I will need to juggle and manage it all independently.

> *If you are searching for balance,*
> *it really isn't just about running faster or*
> *working harder to keep up with all the pieces before*
> *they crash to the ground. That is a recipe for chaos.*
> *It's about simply learning to focus your available*
> *energy every day in the most productive way.*

PHEW! That was a lightbulb moment for me.

Once I started to see how I used my energy throughout the day, and how I could expend it effectively on only what was essential at that moment, everything became so much less stressful. When I used to think about how many tasks I wanted to cram into my available hours of a day or week, I was always running out of time for what really mattered. The only solutions for getting more done in a day seemed to be delegating (a great thing when it is possible), working harder (which made me feel exhausted all the time), or getting less sleep (not so great).

If we focus on how to use our energy well, we can end the day feeling accomplished but not as exhausted. We accomplish so much more with less effort when we devote ourselves to what is essential, eliminate what isn't, and balance how we expend our available energy over a period of time. The best way to be unproductive is to deplete energy by scurrying around feeling frantic all day.

The secret is twofold: Conserve energy by focusing on what is essential in your life, and make time for what refills your energy.

Think of it this way. If you are an introvert, conversation at parties will likely drain your energy. If you want to be energized for a party, you probably feel as if you would need to spend the day practically in silence in order to gear up to enjoy the evening, right? If you don't have the energy to expend on it when the time comes, you will become exhausted immediately and leave early. Or maybe you will end up not even going to the party in the first place. You may decide understandably to stay home altogether so you can curl up in your PJs and read in silence, not because you don't like your friends, but because that peaceful environment is what conserves or refills your energy.

You likely have a long list of things you need to accomplish and a long list of things you would love to fit into your life but never find the time for. Or perhaps you experience the opposite dilemma. You make time for many of the things you love to do but end up disorganized and with very little accomplished in other essential areas of your life.

How you balance each responsibility and priority with the energy you are able to devote to it will determine how accomplished and fulfilled you are at the end of the day.

Do It Now

What are some tasks that tend to drain your energy? How could you rearrange your schedule to give these tasks more focus when you have enough energy for them?

We are all aware that we have energy to use, but when we just charge off into the day we tend to give very little thought for how to harness our energy effectively. You likely have some activities that energize you and some that drain you, and I bet you'll find that it's very hard to focus and make progress on the ones that drain you. Without a plan for how to use our energy well and keep us focused on the essentials, we won't accomplish nearly as much as we need to and have room in our life for what matters to us.

How we use our energy truly does matter!

Stay Motivated

The other day my daughters and I were trying to find our way out of Bellevue. We live in Seattle, and Bellevue is a nice suburb. We had been invited to a Home Depot there to host a workshop and had spent the day in the store. When the workshop was over, we were ready to head back home.

Being new to the area, we consulted that little friend in my iPhone, Siri. For the record, Siri cannot be trusted. But it isn't always her fault. After about six trips in circles around Bellevue, it became clear Siri was totally unaware of construction roadblocks. Siri became frustrated by our wrong turns and tried to reroute us back to where she wanted us to go, and we were downright upset by her insistence that we turn left, because turning left would have caused us certain demise by making us turn onto a freeway in the wrong direction. Eventually, we gave up and went 20 miles the other way so Siri could find us a better route.

It helps to have a road map, but if we plug in the wrong information, we will end up going in circles and cursing when we end up right back where we started. If you are running around aimlessly and find yourself off course, it's time to reset the GPS with the right information and refocus on the most effective way to get where you need to be.

Love It

Shop for a lovely purse-sized notebook and pretty pen to keep in your handbag. Don't be sensible and buy something you won't enjoy using. Find a cute pattern or colorful cover that will inspire you and a pen in a color you like. Use your pretty pen and notebook to jot down ideas that pop into your head when you are out of the house! You never know when inspiration will strike!

If you find yourself relapsing into indecision and holding on to clutter, perhaps after a big life change or setback, give yourself a little pep talk to get back on course. We all need a little refresher now and then to get reinspired, but remember that you already have all the tools you need. You just need to recalibrate your road map. Review the purpose of your home and the mission you are on to make it reflect who you are and what you love. Refocusing will get you out of the rut you've fallen into and back into the groove.

Remember your SMART goals? Sometimes I feel a little lost along the way and start running around in circles because I forget to use my plan. Get a cup of coffee or tea, a notebook, and a pretty pen, and then take a deep breath. The answer of what to do next is always to take the next step. That's why we need our plan out in front of us. Until you get your SMART goal worksheet out and look at it, you'll be wandering around chasing shiny things all day long and wondering why you aren't getting much done. You have to outsmart the chaos and get back on course.

10 Incentives for Staying Focused

1. You'll have more free time to do what you love.

2. You will reach more of your personal and home goals.

3. You'll feel more spontaneous when you want to be.

4. You can enjoy more time with people you love.

5. You'll be more positive about work and life.

6. You'll feel less frazzled every day.

7. You'll be happier and more content with your home.

8. You will be in better financial shape.

9. You will be more organized and prepared.

10. You will be more hospitable to family and guests.

When you find yourself wandering around aimlessly, focus and recalibrate your map. You've got this. Get those gazelle eyes on.

Stop Multi-Focusing

Have you seen the adorable movie *Up*? A little dog in that movie named Dug cracks me up. He'll be meandering around aimlessly, and then suddenly his eyes widen and his head whips around to focus intently on his target, the SQUIRREL! While we normally think about yelling "squirrel!" when we are distracted from what we should be doing, we can think of the squirrel in reverse. Dug's awareness of the squirrel and the intensity with which he focuses on it is a silly illustration of how we can shift our attention from other things on occasion to be fully intent and focused on our prize. For Dug, it was a squirrel. For us, it may be a decluttered and orderly home.

If you feel that you have more to do than hours in the day and never find time for your goals, the trick to succeed in any important but neglected task is to focus on it intently in the period of time you've set aside to do it.

Do It Now

Look around your house. Do you have a project that has been driving you crazy that would take ten minutes or less to complete? Spend some time today finishing it and then celebrate by crossing it off your to-do list.

To find more room in our day for anything important to us, we need to be fully engaged in the most important project or priority in front of us at that time, whether it's spending time with our kids, organizing the hall closet, or writing that book we've always wanted to write. Being focused on one thing at a time doesn't take more time; it just makes us more effective with the time we do have.

Multitasking is effective in some circumstances. If you do dishes and listen to a podcast, for instance, you can do both effectively because the dishes can be done on autopilot. You can take a shower and plan your day or dream up ideas for your next project. You can ride the train to work and write an email. But if you are trying to answer emails and drive the car at the same time, or declutter a closet and make dinner, you'll succeed only at one, or more likely you'll fail or be less efficient at both.

The secret to achieving your goals for a more organized home is to decide which activities need your intense focus so you can stick with those for a designated period of time without distracting yourself at the same time with another task that should have been offered similar focused time. I'm always surprised how much I can accomplish if I set aside focused time on something.

Of course, you can do multiple tasks efficiently throughout the day with a little multitasking, perhaps like cleaning the bathroom and doing laundry by setting a timer to remind yourself to go and remove and fold the clothes from the dryer. But when you try to multi-focus on tasks that needed your undivided attention, everything unravels.

- Focus energy on one important thing at a time. Set a timer for when it's time to move on.

- Focus on your most important work first if possible, for a longer block of time, while your energy and focus will be at its peak.

- Balance your energy with focused blocks of time for daily essentials: what must get done, the domino tasks that will make everything else run more smoothly or be unnecessary, and, of course, don't forget to make room for things that refuel your energy!

- Focus on doing what matters to you each day and be gazelle focused on saving the energy and time to make it happen.

- If you need time to declutter, organize, or work on a project, perhaps swap child care with a friend, or find a "mommy's helper" to come in and watch the kids for a period of time so you can focus all your attention on the task at hand.

The key is to do less, but focus more.

Offering focused attention on each of your priorities at different times of the day will be more productive and energizing than failing at trying to do it all, all at the same time.

Become a Finisher

I used to be the queen of partially completed projects. I was all over the place. I would have just one wall painted, one closet partially organized, or half a room cleaned. In some seasons, that's all the energy or effort I could muster before I had an opportunity to move on to something else. Eventually I may have finished those projects, but usually I was just left with several partially complete ones.

In remodeling, the finishing contractor focuses on all those little details that complete a room. A few years ago I decided I wanted to become a finisher, not just a great starter. When I remodeled the kitchen in my home, I had an opportunity to put that goal into practice. I told myself that, no matter what, I was going to finish that kitchen from top to bottom. Even if I had to get creative with my budget or get help to make it happen, that room was going to be complete. If I was going to set up our dining room, for instance, I wasn't going to stop until it had just what we needed to enjoy that space.

A shift happens in my mind when I set up the goal for myself to be a finisher of a project. Contrary to what you might think, being a finisher isn't about reaching an unrealistic goal of perfection. Finished is different in my mind. Finishing is the art of completion so you can cross something off your list and be fully content with it because there are no dangling projects left to do. Dangling projects are like clutter to me now. I like to complete tasks fully whenever possible.

Finishing a project doesn't mean that suddenly a project has to become expensive or fancy. The very fact that the goal is to be finished often requires using more creativity or substituting what is readily available and realistic instead of what is ideal.

I used to really struggle with finishing a room because I looked at how far I had come and felt that maybe that was far enough, so I would slack off and begin a new project to get that same high from starting something new.

When I decided I was going to commit to *finishing* projects, I had to have a different mind-set. I had to stop patting myself on the back for how far I had come and stop offering excuses for not planning on the finishing details. I had to stop wandering from project to project. To become a finisher, I had to keep my eyes focused on the goal, the end result of my effort.

When I could visualize the project completed—the finished room, the organized closet—I knew what I needed to do to persevere to the end. Finishing a room meant the closet was decluttered and organized, and projects were not just halfheartedly started and abandoned. I didn't stop until there were side tables to set coffee cups, curtains on the windows, a rug on the floor, and lamps on the tables.

You might see a goal of a finished room as rather obsessive, but I see it as freedom because it requires that I not worry about perfection. Finishing a project means I am decluttering my mind of all the petty details that might loom in my head, and I'm streamlining our home so it's efficient for our needs, allowing me to move on to what matters more. A goal of finished projects leaves little room for obsession over perfect details and focuses more heavily on the function of the space.

In order to succeed at any project, from decluttering to making our home more useful for us, we need stay focused on the end result. It's so easy to become distracted or disinterested along the way. When we make that commitment to finish well, it's amazing how priorities start to be shaped. When we *know* we are going to finish, we make better decisions. When we *commit* to finishing, our small daily goals take on new significance. Success won't happen overnight, but with one foot in front of the other, checking items off our task lists, we know we *will* get there!

Pause, Reflect, and Act

Make Room

Do you tend to start projects or have half-completed rooms? Look around at a room or project you would really love to complete. How do incomplete projects or unfinished spaces make you feel? Make a list of things you would like to finish on one room and develop a SMART goal to make it happen!

Let It Go

Make a NOT to-do list! Think about several projects in your home that you would like to do. Now decide which ones should wait! A NOT to-do list will help you to zero in your most important tasks.

Home Love Habit

Practice being a finisher. Work on keeping lists of projects and SMART goals, and add a box you can check off and celebrate when the project is COMPLETE!

7

Create Order

*Organizing is what you do before you do something,
so when you do it, it's not all mixed up.*

CHRISTOPHER ROBIN

As we are decluttering areas of our home and pulling things off shelves to see what we have so we can decide what to keep, consider how difficult we make this process for ourselves when we start to rationalize each piece and how we could cram it back into our closet!

Why is it that we seem to easily see value in our stuff to the point where we might even justify the need for excessive amounts of things crowding our space? What if we were to go about creating order by first weighing the value of the space we have and only bringing in what we have room for? Our closets and cabinets should be seen as prime real estate in our home, special little destinations we can enjoy and protect from chaos.

Honoring the space we have first is a different mind-set for decluttering than evaluating the worthiness of each object to determine what we can keep. It's understandable that we will perceive each item we own as having some worth to us because perhaps we paid a lot of money for it, it has sentimental value, it's appealing to us, or it may be useful or used again in some way in the future.

When we fill each nook and cranny in our home with things we feel are of value (even if we don't really need them right now), we are disregarding how those things impact or diminish the usefulness and value of the space we have. To create order in the house, we need to first consider the beauty and function of our spaces. Then we can more easily create order by determining what and how much we can keep while maintaining the integrity and beauty of the space.

Value Your Space

Sometimes my rooms, and even my furniture, will speak to me. Not exactly in audible words (bless), but I've found that if I pay closer attention to my home and get to know it, I learn things that help me to make better decisions. As long as I'm listening to my house, I find it quite helpful to identify the purpose and name the destinations around my home so I know with whom I am speaking. Now, before you decide I've finally lost it, let me explain. Understanding your space, and what you have space for, will help you make the most sense of what you love.

My daughter Courtney and I were out treasure hunting one day and ran across the prettiest white-painted antique secretary desk and hutch at a secondhand shop. It was tempting, but we didn't think we had a need for it. We boldly walked away (fist pump in the air for willpower!). But it wasn't 20 minutes later (with a Frappuccino in hand this time) that I thought, *That piece was so charming it would be adorable somewhere!* Somewhere in my house, just to be clear.

Soon we found ourselves back in the shop again, gazing at it longingly and dreaming of what we could use it for. We stood in that shop trying to rationalize why we should get it and all the possible places it could sit in our home. (You see, I've learned that I have to avoid bringing furniture into the house unless it will have a distinct purpose and reason to be there. Being just irresistibly cute isn't usually enough of a qualifier. It has to speak to me and explain how it's going to earn its keep!)

Fortunately, that piece was speaking. I could visualize its quaint little desk cubbies filled with notepads and notebooks, and drawers holding cameras and cords, and my favorite books and little treasures lined up tidily behind the glass doors! Not only would it be functional, I knew exactly where it belonged. I had just painted my office with a fresh coat of navy on the walls and put in new hardwood floors to replace the carpet. That was the perfect destination for it.

Besides the new sense of order it would bring to my office, I thought about how the white paint would stand out crisply against the dark blue walls (I'm always smitten by blue and white together) and how the sparkly hardware on the glass doors would feel like jewelry. I knew I'd be inspired to use and enjoy that piece well. Charming? *Check*. Functional? *Check*. Distinct place and purpose for it? *Double check*. The secretary with hutch passed all the tests to come home with me. Now it has a place of honor in my office.

> *When we value a space in our home,*
> *we will love spending time there and taking care of it.*
> *We won't want to clutter it with random things,*
> *or overly stuff it, or neglect it by not using*
> *the space for a distinct and useful purpose.*

We all have spaces in our home we tend to protect naturally. I mean, thankfully most of us don't try to stuff our jeans into the utensil drawer. We just know instinctively that that drawer is for silverware only, not pants. But some spaces in our home seem to attract random clutter, and we get so much excess tucked in that we need to be a bit clearer about what stays and what goes.

Whether it's a corner set up with a chair and a footstool as a delightfully peaceful destination for our morning coffee, or a neat and tidy hall closet that makes finding things a breeze, the way we set up and care for our spaces (and the spaces within those spaces) will help determine what we can keep there.

Know What to Keep and Where to Put It

The two most important decisions you can focus on to bring order to any space are:

1. what to keep
2. where it belongs

Yet in my mind, the rules for exactly what is meant by "what" and "where" can get a little murky if I allow myself too many creative liberties about what exactly the expectations and guidelines are for what I can keep and where it can go.

Take clothes, for instance. Tell me I am not the only one who struggles with this. It should be quite obvious when I have too much. I might spend a lot of time trying to wrangle tangled hangers and in frustrating searches to find the pieces I need. I might feel that I have too many options one day and I can't even decide what to choose, and then feel that I have nothing at all to wear the next day.

I'm a case. I need help.

Don't even get me started on the challenges of paring down and deciding what clothing to keep. I really do have the best intentions of fitting into my favorite pre-baby jeans (although it should be noted in full disclosure that my baby is now 15). Is there a statute of limitations for making a decision on what clothes fit you?

When I am trying to decide what to keep and what to let go of, I'm like a lawyer. I can find loopholes and justifications to allow myself to keep just about anything I want. Just keep what I love? Not strict enough for this girl. I might have lotsa love for those clothes I'm planning on wearing someday when I can fit back into them. I might even have love for enough items to fill three closets, even though I technically only have one.

As I mentioned before, most of us know instinctively that pants do not go in the utensil drawer. No one needs to tell us that. It's an unspoken rule. No amount of logic will convince us that we should make room for the pants with the forks because, you know, random things don't go together. So why not take that obvious logic a step further and apply that rule of appropriateness and all that is right in the world to every other space in our house?

Random things don't go together, so even though we might feel that it is obvious that clothes go in our closet, it can be risky to leave the guidelines so wide. Because, if you are like me, *clothes* is a very broad category with plenty of room for interpretation and misunderstanding about what is allowed.

Things get a little confusing if we do not define the meaning of *clothes*, for instance. Being a little bit more specific about what you mean when you say *clothes*, and what spaces are available for them, will help define what goes where and what does not. And then for good measure, remind yourself of the limitations of your space. Trust me. Even if you are a little more free-spirited about organizing like I am, your closet space and brain space will thank you for the clearer guidelines.

I've come a long way with my clothing organization, and I'm still learning a few tricks. Being ever resourceful and determined to win the war against clutter, I've had to find ways to outsmart myself. Perhaps these tricks will help you think about your space a little more effectively too. Gazelle strategies, activate!

Try defining your spaces in ways that are less open to interpretation. For example,

> *This is a shelf only for sweaters that meet all three of these guidelines: They fit me, I've worn them regularly in the last 12 months, and I fully intend to wear them regularly in the next 12.*

And then give yourself the space restriction in case you are at all prone to overstuffing or hoarding:

> *I can stack four rows of sweaters, three high. That is my sweater-space limit.*

No forks and no pants go here, in case there was any doubt.

Try it again for other areas of your house that tend to get a little bit crazy:

> *Space definition:* This is a cabinet where I put the sheets that fit beds I have, and I will stack pillowcases that are not stained, bleached, or otherwise unappealing to me.

> *Space limitation:* I can have one spare sheet set per bed, no more.

Space definition: This is a drawer for jammies I would not be ashamed to be seen in should the fire department need to rescue me.

Space limitation: I can have 5 pairs of jammies in this drawer, no more.

Now, not all spaces can be as neatly defined by one category per space. You may have to have several categories of items on a shelf or in a drawer, but that's okay. You are the rule maker. You decide what goes together in each space and how the space will be utilized and organized. But here's the one rule you shouldn't break: your own rule. If you make the rule that tank tops and shorts go together in one drawer, tank tops on one side and shorts on the other, do not allow yourself (not even once) to set a tank top on the dresser, on the floor, on your pile of pants, or stuffed in with the sweaters. That's why you need to make the rules for yourself in the first place, so you have a rule to keep.

When you can name the destination and are clear as to what you will find when you get there, it's more obvious what doesn't go where, and you'll have a clearer guideline for what is too much. No pants in the silverware drawer, and no ugly pillowcases or sheets for beds you don't have in the linen closet.

If you ever feel a little uncertain even with your new, better-defined guidelines, ask yourself this: "Will keeping this item or making this decision increase the clutter and chaos or move my space closer toward order and beauty?"

Do It Now

Feeling indecisive about what to keep and what to let go of? Choose to let that thing go. If you ever find a new one that you really love and know you'll use at that time, you can replace it. Otherwise, you probably won't miss it anyway.

Be a Matchmaker

Part of getting organized is simply decluttering and paring down so that organization is easier, but part of the secret to making more room for what you love and enjoying the space you have is to create order in the house.

There is no sense in trying to organize clutter, so it really isn't advantageous to skip the decluttering, but you can make just about anything look tidier. This will probably trouble the minimalists among us, but there are some easy tricks to making your house feel a lot better even before you get around to decluttering all the things.

There really are no universal rules about how much stuff you can have. Remember, you'll determine how much is just enough for you and your space. You may have room for less, and someone else may have room for a little more. But whether it's a little or a lot, what we have usually looks more streamlined when we create order with what we love around us.

Let's start with playing matchmaker and then tidy up the things that go together. If you have things spread out all over the house, you are likely going to feel that things are a little bit chaotic. Set aside some time to bring things together in a more orderly way. You might be surprised by how much better you feel about your space!

Start with these three steps:

1. Like items go together
2. Everything has a home
3. Tidy them up!

Test this out in any room in your house. Do you have magazines on several surfaces around the room or house? Bring them all together in one spot. That spot is their home. It can be a basket, a coffee table, or a lidded box. Remember, no pants there, just magazines. Pare down as you group things together so you only keep what really inspires you. Make sure they are all facing the same way and fit in their home without a few falling out or being too tightly stuffed so that it feels orderly.

Look around your house for magazines you could donate to your doctor's office or hairdresser. Put them in the car to drop them off next time you visit.

Do you have vases in several cupboards around the house, a few in the garage, and some under your sink? Give them just one home. (Vases do not need to have vacation homes. Just one will do.) At this point you'll probably realize you have far too many. Pare them down to what you love, actually have used recently, and will likely use again. Give away the rest, or if you really want to save them for giving flowers from your garden to friends, assign those a new, out-of-the-way home.

You might only have one sock drawer, but when all the sock types and colors are together, it can feel like a mess. I personally don't fold our socks (I'm sorry). They just get tossed in a drawer. But there are some tricks to create more order!

Match up like socks together. Your white sport socks can be on one side of the drawer, and your black dress socks will be all together on the other. Keep tights together and then bring slipper socks together.

When my kids were little, we had the worst time with socks losing their mates. The girls had socks to match outfits and all sorts of fun patterns and colors times two girls. Lots of socks, and yet none would have a mate. Instead of wearing mismatched socks every day (totally an option) or spending precious time trying to match up all the different colors and patterns and sort which ones went into which child's room, we simplified the socks we bought.

From that day forward, my girls had only one kind of white, every-day socks to wear (boring, I know), and our son had only one type of white sock. There was no way to mess this up. We did the girls' laundry together and the boy's laundry separately to make sock sorting even easier.

Items like cleaning supplies can be tricky because they might have several logical homes, but, nevertheless, they should not have more than one home in each space. You have a choice. You can run around the house and bring all of the cleaning supplies together in just one central home (which makes sense so you don't have to buy or maintain order with multiple cleaning supplies and locations), or you can give them several homes where it makes sense for convenience. I personally like to keep cleaning products in each bathroom because I'm far more likely to keep my bathroom clean if it is easy to do so. Go a step further to restore order by corralling the supplies in a bucket or basket so you'll be inspired by order when you open the cabinet.

You can organize your closet for more visual order too. Shirts together, pants together, dresses together. While you can organize by color if that inspires you, items will look especially tidy if each category is grouped by the length of the item.

Try this: Start at the left side of your closet and group the longest dresses together, followed to the right of those by longer skirts, then shirts in order of length, and then pants.

Everything should have a home. When you see a little clutter forming somewhere, it's your job to find it a home. Think of everything you see wandering freely around your house like a lost pup that needs to be reunited with the other pups at its home.

Create Storage Solutions

Having a lot of storage is risky business. The more storage we have available to us, the more stuff we might acquire to fill it, and the harder it becomes to keep track of what we have. For a while, my husband and I had a house that had the most amazing storage space ever. It was technically considered a crawl space, but it was the biggest, nicest, cleanest crawl space you've ever seen. You could fully stand up in it, no crawling necessary. It had an exterior door for easy access to 1,000 square feet of empty and unobstructed storage. A dream, right? We thought so too.

Every time we faced a decision on what to do with something we really didn't have room for in the house, my husband and I looked at each other with a twinkle in our eyes because...STORAGE! Off it went, under the house. For years we saved ourselves from the inconvenience or trouble of making a decision on what to do with things because we didn't have to. We had more than enough room for just about anything to stay.

We weren't paying any extra to keep it, and I didn't even have to look at it! It was out of my house but clean, dry, and organized for when we wanted it. Stuff stored under the house seemed like such a good idea until we had to move out and realized the error of our ways. We were suddenly forced to make a million decisions all at once, and we ended up giving away almost everything we had hung on to all those years over just a few short days. I felt a little guilty that other people could have been enjoying our stuff all that time. Oh, well. Lesson learned. We cannot be trusted with that much storage.

I was a crawl space hoarder.

In spite of the potential pitfalls of too much storage or the temptation to disguise clutter by putting it in a pretty container, getting organized with designated storage and having systems that help you to find what you need are very good things. For those of us who love having pretty things we use, an organizational system is what is going to keep our home from appearing cluttered. A simple system will also make it more likely that we will be able to find what we love so we can use it.

What we don't want is to see everything we love all out on display at once. Even if we love all the things, seeing them sitting around is just too much. Your belongings should blend into the background to inspire you, not overwhelm you.

> *Storage should do its job behind the scenes to keep*
> *belongings contained and organized so we can focus*
> *on living our lives and enjoying our space.*

The goal with things we love is to declutter, get organized, and containerize so we can get on with living and using what we love. Without storage and designated spots for everything, we will always be doing battle with stuff! Getting organized is fun!

Clearly, storage containers should be a support to your sense of order, not just a way to hide a clutter habit. Organized storage spaces will make your life more efficient and help you to use your space efficiently. If you are fortunate enough to have a house full of built-ins and ample closets and storage areas, you can feel organized by giving each built-in space a purpose and then putting things away. That is wonderful! But if you do not have all the built-ins or closets you want or need, you can get creative by gathering furniture, baskets, and hooks to help you get organized.

We want to avoid complicated systems because if they don't make sense to us or if they make us have to think or remember things, we will struggle to keep up with our system. Everything should have a designated home that makes sense and is effortless to use.

How and where to store seasonal decor or various holiday items is definitely an issue for creative types who enjoy the festivity of the holidays and decorating for the seasons. I've never been quite as into specific holiday-themed decorating as some, but I do like to acknowledge each season and bring it into my home somehow. Paying attention to the seasons and evolving my house creatively is how I feel more connected to my home and stay content with what I have year-round, so finding ways to incorporate those items is important to me.

You should feel free to be creative in your home. Please don't feel that seasonal decor should be banished from your space just because some might find it frivolous or unnecessary. Keep what you love, and use and enjoy it!

While I keep my seasonal decorating to mostly natural items, such as plants, branches in vases, fruit and veggies in bowls, or things I might find in the yard, such as pinecones or flowers, I do love letting my home evolve with the seasons in other ways that require storage. I love to have seasonal textiles and table decor too. I enjoy bringing out the plaid table runner in the fall and the striped one in the summer. I might have a few pillow covers to change out. I even have a set of gray lampshades for the winter and replace them with white for summer (too much?). Those simple changes are fun to me.

As long as I have the space for them and am not overwhelmed by it, creative freedom in my home is truly enjoyable. Because built-in storage isn't always an option, I collect sturdy, lidded baskets to hold certain things I love to use for entertaining throughout the year, such as candles and accessories I might use in one season or another. I keep them grouped together by category (textiles, for instance) in the room that makes the most sense (dining room or living room).

Organizing my table candles, pinecones, or seasonal table decor in just two or three lidded baskets stacked together in a corner of the dining room or below a console table is an effortless and easy-to-implement system. It makes sense, doesn't take up much room, and is simple to keep up with.

It doesn't even always make sense to me to take the time to record everything in each basket if I can quickly look through all three baskets in a matter of moments, where keeping up with a list means I have to remember to keep it updated and then remember where I put my list. But if you have a lot of small things organized in baskets and want to be more detailed and systematic, you might want to keep a list on your phone or taped inside the basket. Do what makes you feel better and what is enjoyable!

Alternatively, if you have the space available, you can set up a seasonal shelving unit in the garage or basement, or even use a cabinet in the house where all your seasonal pieces and decor are located. No matter what system you use for keeping things you love to use organized, make sure it makes sense to you and is effortless to get to.

Containers strategically placed around the house, such as pretty baskets and boxes with lids, can be an attractive addition to the room while keeping little accessories and necessities hidden to streamline the space. Be mindful of items you bring in and where you put them so they fit seamlessly into your decor rather than clutter your look.

Remember to only bring in containers for what you really need and use in that space, not so many that your clutter multiplies in sneaky ways.

Nine Easy Storage Options to Consider and Tips to Use Them Efficiently

1. Lidded boxes, baskets, and small trunks. Keep an eye out for lidded boxes and small trunks at flea markets, garage sales, or local shops. I have a small, patterned box with a hinged lid on my nightstand for phone cords, notepads, and any other random things I need in my room; another one on my desk for my labeling machine, stapler, and hole punch; and another on a bookshelf near the dining room for extra drinking glasses. Give your family a small trunk to stash all those game controllers and cords so your TV area stays neat and tidy!

2. *Tall open baskets.* Larger, tall, open baskets can be attractive for extra throw blankets or even to toss in extra bed or throw pillows when you are sitting or sleeping.

3. *Small open baskets.* Don't let your pantry look cluttered and feel disorganized. Small open baskets are perfect for grouping pantry items to give you a streamlined and clutter-free pantry or cabinet while making it easier to find what you want at a glance! I have a baking basket in my pantry. When the urge to bake strikes, I can easily grab it and find all the little baking items I need, such as baking powder, baking soda, vanilla, almond extract, salt, and measuring spoons.

4. *Back of the door organizer.* Get organized without taking up additional space by adding door-organizing systems. Find space for gift wrap, office supplies, pantry goods, shoes, bathroom necessities, office supplies, craft items, paper, art supplies, cards, and more.

5. *Desk organizers, bulletin boards, file drawers.* Use desk organizers to keep essentials organized and attractive. Hang a bulletin board to pin and contain important reminders, notes, or inspirational images. Organize important papers with file folders in drawers or file boxes. Use drawers, cabinets, and storage boxes to group office supplies.

6. *Pegboard organizers.* For keeping small, everyday tools such as screwdrivers, hammers, and picture hangers organized, make your own pegboard organizer for the garage or other convenient location. You can find pegboard, hooks, and organizers at home improvement stores.

7. *Wire baskets.* A wire basket is an attractive way to corral wayward items on an entry table (mail or school papers or things to return), as well as the perfect addition to a kitchen counter to hold your pretty hand towels.

8. *Large baskets.* Have a large basket in or near the entry to toss in shoes or for outside accessories, such as hats and scarves, or for pets,

such as their raincoats (yes, our dogs have raincoats for rainy days), harnesses, or flashlights for nighttime walks.

9. *Under-the-sink storage.* The space under the sink is often underutilized and disorganized. Utilize the vertical space by adding stackable drawers, shelf risers, or adjustable units specifically made to fit around sink pipes. Fill the drawers or shelves with cleaning supplies under the kitchen or laundry sink, and cosmetics and toiletries under the bathroom sink.

The goal with storage solutions is for them to be functional and beautiful. You'll enjoy maintaining the organization much more, and you'll be much happier to see storage throughout your house if it is a part of your style rather than just unattractive plastic bins that gather clutter and dust!

What kinds of items tend to clutter up your house? After you pare down what you have, how could you solve organizational issues by finding a home for things?

Pause, Reflect, and Act

Make Room

How could you find more joy in the space you have? Take a walk around your house and look at closets and rooms. Are you honoring and making the most of the rooms you have, or are they filled with too much stuff? How could you pare down to better reflect the space you have to love your home even more?

Let It Go

Grab a bag and go on a decluttering mission. Make it a goal to pare down 50 percent of surfaces to give them room to breathe. Focus on getting rid of items you would not buy again if you didn't already own them.

Home Love Habit

Develop an eye for order. When you see closets or cabinets that are untidy, take a few moments to restore order by grouping like items and straightening wayward pieces.

8

Offer Grace

By wisdom a house is built,
and through understanding it is established;
through knowledge its rooms are filled
with rare and beautiful treasures.

PROVERBS 24:3-4

We are often our own worst enemy when it comes to feeling inadequate about our ability to manage our home. Will we ever get it to look consistently tidy, well organized, and pretty like the home of our dreams? Or are we just one of those people who will never get it together or have what other people seem to have?

Perhaps you wonder how you can be so desirous of a beautiful, orderly home, and yet have at times such disastrous results along the way! I'm shaking my head laughing, not at you, but because I also wonder that about myself. To be honest, I want to be a person who can live gracefully with imperfection, but I don't always like it when the opportunity arises. All the visions of loveliness that dance in our heads when we look to where we want to be can be the spark that will inspire our goals and light a fire under us to get going, but dreams of how wonderful things would be, if they were perfect for us, can rob us of finding joy right where we are.

If your home is tiny and you scarcely have room for anything you really love, or your budget is small and the potential to change things seems out of reach, rest assured that while there may be a wide divide between the ultimate visions you have for your home and what it looks like right now, this in-between place where you live is enough. There's always a silver lining to be found.

In our heart of hearts we don't want to drain our precious energy by beating ourselves up, experiencing frustration over what we can't do, or spinning our wheels on all the wrong things.

When you find yourself trying hard and then falling fast in making progress in your goals, and you feel as if you just might never arrive where you want to be because perhaps you just don't have what it takes right now, don't worry! When a home is out of control, or things feel chaotic around us, or personal conflicts and challenges are in our life, often our first reaction is to react in a way that brings more stress to the situation.

Each day will undoubtedly present its own unexpected and uninvited challenges, so to avoid the unnecessary time and energy wasted on things we cannot control, we must make a decision in advance for how we will respond to those ups and downs and disappointments. There will always be unwelcome things trying to take control of our heart, mind, soul, and physical surroundings, but we can more easily maintain our composure and find contentment with what we have if our perspective is not on temporal things.

How do we go from focusing on all of the stuff that weighs us down to inviting more grace to fill our rooms?

What exactly is grace? I looked up some definitions, and each one swept me off my feet. I may not always have the most organized home around, but when I focus on creating a home filled with grace, my home is transformed and I can find everything I need.

Grace is:

- a simple elegance or refinement of movement
- a controlled, polite, and pleasant way of behaving
- thoughtfulness toward others

- behaving in a polite way in social situations
- the free and unmerited favor of God and the bestowal of blessings
- an act or instance of kindness, courtesy, or clemency
- a charming or attractive trait or characteristic
- a pleasing appearance or effect

What might our home feel like if we made more room for grace?

Thrive in the Season You Are In

We can grow resentful and discontent with what we have when we are only look-ahead people. I know I'm guilty of that. I'm often a few steps (or light-years) ahead of myself in plans and dreams, looking forward to the next season, the next house, the next adventure, the next project.

Being a look-ahead person can be great for dreaming and goal setting, but for project completion and contentment right here in this moment, we need to be present and make room for plenty of grace.

I love this quote from T.S. Eliot: "Only those who risk going too far can possibly find out how far they can go."

While we might often have a desire to live in a slower world and find a rhythm of living at a more manageable pace, sometimes we just have a lot going on at once. It's hard to feel present when so many things are changing and swirling around us, isn't it? Whether it's by our choosing or the unexpected, we don't always have the ideal circumstances for creating a perfect home. While striving to invite more of what we love into our life, we may even have some unhinged moments as we adjust to the turbulence of change. If we never dream, never change, never try new things, never make room for things we are passionate about, and never, ever risk taking on too much, we will never know how far we might go.

We all have times in life when things go a little bonkers or spiral into a crazy cycle. Change happens. Did you just have a baby? Start a new job or business? Get married? Move to a new house? Experience something stressful? Do you manage many children? Do you battle health or emotional issues or live with people who do?

Even if we haven't been in a season of transition or stress, sometimes we are in a season of slump where we are uninspired. I find myself there sometimes too. Each change, every step backward, and every forward motion is an opportunity to practice and offer grace.

Do It Now

What are your most ungraceful moments at home? Make a list of three things that make you feel disorganized or even just plain ol' crabby in your day. How could you remedy these clumsy moments with simple solutions? Put three solutions on your project list, and make it a goal to fix at least one ungraceful situation this week.

Every time I move into a new home, I imagine we'll be all set up, remodeled, walls repainted, closets organized, and ready to host the neighborhood Christmas party within a few weeks. By December I've lowered my expectations from party hosting to just hoping I'll be able to create a safe path through the garage so we can look for our ornaments. And by February I am a bit discouraged that we haven't painted a single wall, but on the bright side, at least we know what drawer we keep our measuring spoons in so we can finally bake some cookies. Three years later, we might hit our groove. Everything takes a bit longer than I wish it would. As a look-ahead person, I can grow impatient that I'm not further along. That's how it was in our past moves, but I'm hoping I've learned lessons going forward that have changed my perspective.

Soon after I moved into my home, I created a printable list of the definitions of grace. I taped it on my mirror as a gentle but beautiful reminder of where I'm really headed with this home. Yes, I want to declutter my house and organize everything. Having just moved in, in many ways I feel behind, as if I'm starting all over again from scratch even though moving is an understandable circumstance for chaos. I have to learn about this house, how we live here, and where our belongings fit into the structure of this home.

Moving gracefully is an art a dancer works toward for her entire career, but I can't say I always move into new houses with grace. I feel clumsy, awkward, and challenged at times just trying to find my way. Grace takes practice, dedication, and devotion to the art of forward motion in spite of challenges or difficulty. If being graceful requires forward motion, I won't succeed by being so paralyzed by the pressure that I don't take steps in the right direction.

Keeping my eyes focused on increasing the presence of grace even in the more difficult or busy seasons helps my goals for my home become more refined.

- I want a home that reflects simplicity with grace rather than complicated chaos.

- I want to strive for controlled order as a way of life, not just drown in chaos and calamity.

- I want to set reasonable expectations so I am content and pleasant to be around.

- I want to create room in my home and schedule to make more time to be thoughtful of others.

- I want to be a polite hostess who cares about people more than perfection.

- I need to accept that I'm right where I should be, and I'm blessed to be here in this imperfect house.

- I will look for the lessons to be learned in an in-between season.

- I want to remember to accept grace for the mistakes and imperfection but still move forward gracefully toward the reward of being faithful to my mission for my home.

- I want to use each room in my home as an opportunity for kindness and to show courtesy to those who live here.

A home filled with grace and love will be charming and attractive in spite of its imperfections.

Embrace the season you are in and thrive in it gracefully. That is a worthy goal, is it not? Do what you can today with grace. A home should be a sanctuary, but if you try to live in it with unrealistic expectations (for yourself, your spouse, your children, or your home), you are going to slowly destroy whatever peace your home can offer you. As the winds of change blow through or threaten to topple you over, build your home a little stronger each year so it can weather the storms. It's your attitude, your heart, and the joy you bring to your home that will transform it in the most graceful way in every season.

Be Poised and Prepared

Tell me something. When a neighbor rings the doorbell in the middle of a day to ask for a cup of sugar, do you gracefully open the door, warmly smiling because you feel totally poised, pulled together, fully dressed (yes, pants on), and teeth brushed? Or is it your first instinct to slip quietly around the corner and hide, hoping they will give up and go away? Wouldn't it be lovely to run into a friend outside when you are getting your mail and welcome her inside for a chat without a moment of fear that she will trip or injure herself simply making her way to the living room?

Do It Now

Look around your home. If you were to invite a friend over right now, what would be the most important area to you to have cleaned up to honor her arrival? Clean or tidy up that area right now as a gift to yourself.

We all have different comfort levels with inviting others into our home when we are not fully prepared for or expecting their arrival. Our home is our sanctuary, after all, and not a public place, but even more important than fearing how others might perceive us or function in our home when they visit is the thought-provoking question of how we feel in our very own space.

Is our home set up in such a way that we can move about gracefully in our daily tasks, or have we inadvertently set up obstacles at every turn, making what should be an effortless experience, such as leaving the house, awkward and frustrating? To live more gracefully and find joy in the experience of creating a home, we need to remove those pesky annoyances that make us feel unprepared and hinder us from being effective.

How effortlessly are we are able to move about our home, tidying up and completing daily tasks? We might try to convince ourselves that piles of clutter are the evidence that we are relaxed and comfortable with our surroundings, but how can we fully feel at ease if we are constantly missing crucial deadlines due to lost papers, if we are late to appointments because we could not find our keys, if we have to leave the house looking frazzled because we have to put on our shoes and coat as we are making our way out the door because they were not where they belonged?

We cannot help but feel clumsy when our floors are covered with clutter and our tables are piled high with delayed decisions still waiting to be handled. If we are annoyed with everyone around us as we go about cleaning the house, it's likely because tasks have been procrastinated until each one now feels unbearable.

When we are more organized and prepared for daily tasks, and when we can set up our spaces to avert the predictable mishaps that always result in chaos, we can feel more poised and graceful at home.

When we are more prepared, we can enjoy the simple pleasures of puttering around our house, tidying up each day. The stress we used to experience in getting ready for the day starts to melt away. Instead of routinely running out the door and causing a big commotion by yelling, slamming doors, uttering unmentionable words, or getting in the car angry because once again we are going to be late, we can walk out at a leisurely pace, poised and prepared for the day.

Do a little experiment. Get yourself a pretty notepad (yes, I like to offer you lots of opportunities to make use of those pretty notepads!) and set it near your front door, on your fridge, or in your purse. For the next week, every time you or someone in your family experiences frustration in the house, jot down a note of what caused that experience. Don't write WHO was at fault, but rather WHAT. Misplaced coat? Missing homework assignment? No clean socks in the drawer? No spoon for their cereal? No logical place to put something? Needing to dig through big piles of clutter for lost items?

On another sheet, start to form logical solutions to the problems. Then, put each one on your to-do list.

When our family moved into our new house, we experienced frustration every day simply because we didn't have hooks anywhere. We had grown so accustomed to using our systems at our old house that we felt quite ungraceful moving about the new one. We wandered around uncertain where to put our purses, our sweatshirts, and our coats; our shopping bags with things to return; or our towels. Far too many things ended up piled on floors, tossed over chairs, and hanging on door-knobs, making locating our belongings challenging and navigating to our closets a risky experience. All of those items needed a home, and a hook was an easy solution!

The longer we procrastinate on setting up our home to function for us, the more we will feel clumsy and disorganized. What is stopping you from finding solutions to your daily frustrations around the home? What are some solutions you could implement so you can move about more gracefully?

Imagine the state of your mind when you head out, if rather than leaving frazzled, you spent the last 30 minutes calmly picking up toys and doing the dishes while listening to some lovely music with a candle going! You'll probably walk out feeling confident, put together, and, dare I say, graceful.

How to Get Organized with Hooks

I have a bit of an addiction. I'm hooked on hooks! Hooks are a perfect solution for getting day-to-day items such as coats, bags, and towels off the floor, and they add instant character to a room too! Hooks are an easy home base for many things, so see if you can find ways to incorporate them all over your home.

In the entry. Every entry needs a few hooks! A coat closet is handy for hiding clutter but not as easy to use for frequently used items. Coat closets seem to be perpetually cluttered and often too small for our needs, so hooks can increase your usable hanging space for coats, purses, leashes, and almost anything that needs to be carried in and out of a house in a tote bag!

In the bathroom. Give each family member a hook with a number on it (or hang a house number above it) so they have a designated spot for their own towel or whatever they need to hang there while they are getting ready, such as a robe or cosmetic bag.

In the kitchen. Hang hooks on the sides of cabinets or kitchen islands to hold a dishtowel, hand towel, or oven mitt. If you are tight on storage space, hooks can be hung for pans and cooking utensils too. Hang a few small hooks under the sink for cleaning rags or other necessities to get things off the floor of the cabinet. Keep your keys on a hook in the kitchen so they have a designated home.

How we feel in our own space IS connected to how we feel when we get outside of it. It's apparent. We can't separate the two.

Interestingly, as we remove the obstacles in our home that make us feel clumsy and put in their place simple systems to help us to feel more graceful, it's quite likely we will become more gracious to others as well.

Have an Attitude of Gratitude

Each room in our home offers us an opportunity to reclaim the space and make more room in it for what we really want.

We can practice grace, increase gratitude, and make our home more beautiful by changing how we look at each room. Rather than seeing our space as a storage room for a random assortment of things, consider it a place to nurture people and create experiences.

Your kitchen is a place to nurture your family. As you prepare the food, clean the counters, and empty the sink each day, make a habit of doing that with gentle care and thankfulness rather than just frustration for the repetitiveness of the chore. Establish an atmosphere of gratefulness, grace, and love for the people who gather there.

Is your family's dining table covered with papers and clutter every day? You can establish a daily practice of thankfulness by creating an inviting gathering space! Clear the clutter, make that space pretty, and gather at the table. Look at each face and say a prayer of gratitude for the gifts around the table. See your table as a sacred space where you offer nourishment to those you love, and you'll find tidying it a soothing ritual every day.

Your bedroom should be a place to refresh and renew each day. Clutter and disorganization steal peace and distract you from the rest and solitude you need. Set aside time to tidy with gratitude that you have this space to recharge.

There are simple shifts we can make in our perspective to bring more gratitude into our home. Quite a few years ago, when my kids were younger, we came up with a list of 20 little attitudes of gratitude for our home. These little reminders inspired us to focus on our blessings:

1. Mind your manners. Say "please," "thank you," and "excuse me."

2. Smile when you see your family. Turn your frown upside down.

3. Pick up after yourself.

4. Notice when others do kind things for you, and show gratitude by action or words.

5. Say "I love you" before going to bed.

6. Give hugs daily.

7. Don't worry about tomorrow. Focus on what you are happy about today.

8. Create gratitude journals to keep track of daily blessings.

9. Show thankfulness for even the little things others do for you.

10. Leave love notes in unexpected places, like lunch boxes and under pillows.

11. Encourage someone with a compliment.

12. Verbalize what you are grateful for when you feel like complaining.

13. Keep a basket of small slips of paper on the table. Write notes of thankfulness during the week and read them to each other during a family meal.

14. Remember to thank God for blessings each day.

15. Surprise your family (or friends) with little gifts or treats to show you thought of them.

16. No grumbling about minor annoyances around the house.

17. Do special things to cherish time with your family. You never know what tomorrow will bring.

18. Reflect on happy memories regularly. Make inspiration boards of special times.

19. Help someone out without them having to ask you. Watch for someone in need.

20. When you are doing household chores, be grateful you have a home to clean.

I encourage you to list each room in your home and create a mission statement for bringing more gratitude to the space.

Love It

Set up an inspiring area in your home with note cards, colored pens, and stamps to send thank-you cards or notes of encouragement to friends. You can set up a space in a cabinet you love, in a pretty box with a lid, or even in a brass letter holder on your desk.

Offer Gracious Hospitality

Part of showing gratitude for what we are blessed to have is including those things in our life. If we truly love something, it should bring us joy. What's the point in having anything if we just hide it away in storage and never use it?

For example, part of my love language and expression of gratitude is inviting people into my home. I love putting together centerpieces and place settings that create a welcoming ambience for the people around my table. For a while I had entertaining supplies such as napkins, napkin rings, serving utensils, candleholders, and runners I could use, but those things were never easy to find or access. When they were stashed somewhere, napkin rings in one area of the house and napkins in another and candlesticks stuck perhaps in a long-lost bin somewhere out in the garage, I didn't use them. I actually dreaded the thought of rummaging all over the house to find things and was sad when setting a table meant I couldn't find the pieces I really loved.

One day I had an epiphany. If setting those pretty tables brought so much joy to my life, creating ambience was an opportunity to be a more gracious hostess. I needed to bring those entertaining supplies together and give them a place of honor where they could be used and enjoyed.

Soon after I found two new, shallow cabinets that had enough space for some table accessories and pretty cloth napkins, a little drawer with enough room for my napkin rings, and a drawer for my favorite candlesticks. I went through my house gathering all of the special pieces I loved to use on my table and brought them together where I could find them.

Once I brought in those simple storage elements and put the system in place to hold the things I loved, guess what? I found myself entertaining more and experiencing more gratitude for that gift.

Love It

Gather items in a basket or cabinet that you can bring out when you want to set up a special meal for family and when entertaining friends. Find cloth napkins in fun patterns or make them out of fabric. Include a set of pretty drinking glasses. Collect dessert or salad plates to dress up your everyday dishes. Gather unscented, colored candles and unique candlesticks.

We all long to feel welcome, cared for, and included, don't we? A home can offer us a safe haven from the world, but it also can be a place to welcome others in to be a part of our life. You know when you go to an open house that is for sale and the owner or Realtor has cleaned the house and baked cookies so the whole house smells amazing? They are luring you in, hoping you'll feel welcome and at home. They want you to feel as if you really belong there! It's a great strategy. Our first home smelled delicious!

When my house is tidy and clean and good smelling, I'm hoping it helps everyone to feel welcome and wanted in this space. Clutter and chaos might make you feel like your home is lived in, but it can also make you feel unsettled and less hospitable. Not only might you feel ashamed of the mess or disorder and be less likely to welcome guests in, but those you are welcoming might feel that they weren't expected or they are intruding in your personal space.

Obviously, we hope our friends will come to see us, not how tidy our house is. It's ultimately about the connection to people, not the state of the house. But when you are hosting a special party to which you have invited guests, you might find you will relax more when the day arrives and your guests will feel extra welcomed into a space because you have prepared it with them in mind.

The goal for me in being a hostess isn't *entertaining* people (because let's be honest, I'm not all that talented or funny), but rather setting up the time and experience for *meaningful connection* to take place.

Have fun inviting guests to your home and making the experience special.

What are some ways you could begin to reset the atmosphere of your home this season to make room for gratitude and hospitality?

Pause, Reflect, and Act

Make Room

To be a more gracious person, it helps to be prepared. What is one thing you've always wanted to do in order to be more hospitable or gracious to a friend? Perhaps you'd like to set up a guest bedroom, or send greeting cards to people to show you care. How could your home be better set up to make you a more gracious friend?

Let It Go

You don't have to live with things as they are, even if you are responsible for how they are! If you have a room or a space that doesn't function well or inspire you to love it because you didn't make the right choice for furniture or colors or style, or you've neglected to make the right decisions in any way, don't punish yourself anymore. Find someone to bless with things you don't need and make new choices so you'll love where you live.

Home Love Habit

There's always a long list of things to do, but how could you focus more on gratitude for what you've already done and what you have right in front of you? Make an "I Am Thankful For..." journal, and every time you feel overwhelmed, turn it into a moment of gratitude. Dirty sheets to wash? Be grateful for a washing machine. Dishes to do? Be grateful for food on those plates. A mess in the living room? Be grateful for family. Unfinished projects? Be grateful for opportunities. Long to-do list? Be grateful as you reflect on what you've already accomplished.

9

Enjoy Luxury

If you wait for perfect conditions,
you will never get anything done.

ECCLESIASTES 11:4 TLB

Is *luxurious* a word you would use to describe your home? It wouldn't be the first word that popped into my head to describe my house or even my family. We are pretty laid-back, casual, and budget-friendly people.

The dictionary defines *luxury* as the state of great comfort or ease and extravagant living. *Luxury* is synonymous with *splendor* and *magnificence*.

Extravagant living might sound a little over the top, but I wouldn't be upset if my house was set up that way simply because it would provide us with great comfort and ease and enjoyment of living.

If we live with excessive material belongings, or perhaps acquire and keep an abundance of stuff we don't need or even enjoy simply because we can be extravagant, that seems to me to be indulgent.

If we have closets that are filled with too many clothes and a house stuffed with belongings we don't use, we are not living with comfort or ease but rather excess—and we may start to appreciate very little of it without even realizing it.

So when I think of living among little luxuries, I think of making room for the simple pleasures one can find in enjoying something very special. To be special and luxurious, it needs to stand out. It should be pleasant and satisfying, but that doesn't mean it's lavish or expensive.

We can feel a *sense of luxury* simply by considering and limiting what items we will allow to inhabit our home and taking care with how we present those items. As we pare down the excessive stuff we keep and manage, life feels more luxurious. When we have simplified what we have, we have a more heightened enjoyment of what remains.

Perhaps this sounds indulgent, but within my own budget and ability, I decided long ago that I wanted my home to feel like more than just an ordinary house. I want to create a restful retreat, a special destination that comforts my family and prepares us with the energy and inspiration to impact the world outside of it.

Don't you want your home to feel like an escape from the world too? Do you dream of a cozy nest to return home to? A comfortable place to nestle in away from the storms of life? Shouldn't a home be a place to feel pampered and taken care of when you need a little love?

If what we are creating is a retreat, why not make it as beautiful, comfortable, and peaceful as possible? Who really wants to create a place so crazy, cluttered, and disorganized that it is more of a place you want to escape from?

Yes, life can be crazy at home. As long as we live there, messes will exist. But, remember, you get to decide the ambience you want to set for your home and life. You get to decide the overall trajectory for the design of your home and how you want it to feel. You get to decide how you want your home to impact your life. You get to decide what little luxuries you want to indulge in at home. But no matter how frugal and sensible you and your choices might be, I hope you'll endeavor to make room for your home to feel special to you in as many ways as possible.

With each decision you make to be more selective in your choices and pare down to the best of what you love, you'll find that your home will become more luxurious even on a less-than-fancy budget.

Savor What You Have

Because being buried with excess and overwhelmed by clutter will feel anything but magnificent, the goal in truly appreciating luxury isn't to keep everything we have and even try to squeeze in a little more, but rather to pare down to just what we need and love. We want to keep the best and shed the rest. Now, that does not mean we should "keep the best and put the rest in a shed." I mean, take a hard look at what you have and trim it down until you have the best you can have right now!

We do not experience luxury by the quantity of things we keep, but rather by the quality of the experiences we have in our home. To feel connected to our home, we have to find ways to savor it.

How might you begin to select quality over quantity around the house? You may not think of some items as luxurious, but imagine a home where every cabinet was filled with only what was needed. Imagine that everything you have works well, is easy to find, and can be more fully appreciated because your home isn't one of excess.

- You might pare down many random serving or baking dishes that you don't use or care for, but keep the ones you use the most and like, your very best ones.

- If you have a huge stash of magazines, you might pare down to the ones with your favorite covers or spreads inside, or go a step further and tear out the specific pages you are inspired by and put them in a binder of inspiration.

- Your kids might have tons of colorful markers, but many are worn out, so art projects are not as enjoyable. Keep the markers that work and toss the ones that don't.

- You know all those things you save in multiples because they might come in handy? The travel mugs, the water bottles, the lunch boxes, the Tupperware. How many of any of these things do you really ever use at one time? Keep the favorites and donate the rest.

- Pare down to only the hand lotions you love and want to use.

- Don't keep every plastic bottle and soap dispenser on the counter. Just leave out the most attractive items.

- Rather than keeping multiple specialty items that have been cluttering up your cabinets, pare down to just a few kitchen gadgets you actually enjoy using. Maybe you don't need to have a rice cooker, the Ninja Blender, a Magic Bullet, a Nutribullet, a panini press, a cake pop maker, waffle maker, an ice cream machine, a donut maker, a bagel toaster, and a toaster oven. Consider if the benefit of owning all of those items is really adding to the quality of your life on a daily basis because you use them or if they are just filling up space in your kitchen.

Pare down so that you have *room* for the best and room to *collect* the best!

Do It Now

Do you have a crowded storage area or cabinet in your home you could make more luxurious and inviting? Get rid of surplus or duplicate items, remove broken items, and donate good items you just don't need. Make this space special with paper-lined shelves and breathing room to showcase only the best of the best.

As you are making your way around your house increasing little luxuries and decreasing the quantity of clutter, you'll want to also pay more attention to what you buy and bring into your home.

In the past you might have bought excess things, hoping to make a bigger statement with quantity or wanting to have more options. Now the goal is to be more selective about what comes in. Think carefully before you buy. Is this something that will enhance the quality of your life at home or will it soon join all the clutter in the spare room?

Will this new item be enjoyable to own, or will it cause what you already have to appear less special because you are simply increasing the quantity of items? Don't spend money on something temporary that you don't love just to fill a space or to have something new.

You don't have to have expensive or fancy things to set the mood. The ambience you create is actually in how you present and use the things you do have. You might have a home furnished with yard sale finds or things you've picked up at a discount store, but if your home is clean, decluttered, and carefully styled with the best of what you've collected over time, it can feel just as luxurious as a house filled with more expensive items.

Setting the Stage for Luxury

Try this. Clear clutter off your counter and wipe it down with a hot, sudsy rag. Looks better already, doesn't it? Now for the fun part. Put back only what is lovely and feels intentionally placed for your enjoyment. Near the stove place a pretty bottle of olive oil, a set of glass salt and pepper shakers, and a crock with wooden spoons. Step back to admire how luxurious and attractive those items are!

We savor more of what we have when we've been selective about what we keep. Clutter often prevents us from appreciating what we already have. A lack of appreciation may even confuse us to mistakenly think we need something better. When we know we have special things to use in our home, we look forward to enjoying them as we use them. When we look forward to using special things, we take better care of them as being something of value to us.

As we pare down to quality over quantity, something peculiar happens. We suddenly have more space in our cabinets. We might even have empty drawers. There is breathing room around the things we love. As tempting as it might be to see empty spaces as an invitation to get more things, don't rush to fill those spaces. Savor them. Room to breathe feels luxurious, don't you think?

One of the best ways to heighten our awareness of the blessings around us is to indulge our senses in as many ways as possible. When we have less distractions and clutter competing for our attention, suddenly we become more aware of what we enjoy. When we are rushing around frazzled, we miss out on the finer details of an experience. We have to slow down to savor what we have. Slow down and elevate each experience to something more indulgent and memorable by incorporating the scents, sights, sounds, and textural experiences you enjoy.

When you become aware of the things that impact you in a positive way, you're able to pay more attention to those things and remember their significance.

Treat Yourself Right

Picture the ambience of a little boutique clothing shop you love. When you stop in, the music is enjoyable and the store smells delicious. I bet you see only the very best products folded neatly on the shelves. Everything is within reach, and nothing is stacked too high. You can select clothes arranged in your favorite colors and patterns with ease because they are hung with breathing room between them on attractive matching hangers. Even if you don't buy anything, you love going in that shop to browse because being in that place is a luxurious experience!

Ten Ways to Make Your Bed Luxurious

1. Invest in a set of luxury-quality sheets.

2. Perhaps save money on an inexpensive duvet and duvet cover, but splurge on lovely velvet Euro pillows.

3. Make your bed every day. You'll feel pampered when you return home to it later.

4. Fold up a cozy blanket across the end of the bed.

5. Prop up your pillows against the wall or headboard and fluff them to look their best.

6. Clear off your nightstands, add a plant, small bud vase, or a favorite candle.

7. Turn on a lamp for a warm, inviting, and luxurious glow.

8. Open a window slightly to let in some fresh air.

9. Set a rug under your bed or a small rug next to your bed for a soft place to set your feet in the morning.

10. Install dimmer switches for ambience.

Now think about those clothing stores designed to draw in the teenagers. (You know the ones I'm talking about.) They have intense, booming music, and the clothes are always halfway hanging off the hangers and packed in too tight to get anything out, so a lot of things end up on the floor. All the racks are packed so close together that you can hardly get through them without knocking things down. You have to hunt through a bunch of junk, 90 percent of which you don't really like, but when you do find something you want, you try to grab it, but the entire shelf collapses under the weight of all the excess. After causing a big commotion and setting off security alarms, you can't wait to get out of there. That entire experience feels chaotic, doesn't it?

If you set up your own closet to be as tidy and inspiring as a beautiful boutique, imagine how at peace you would feel when you got dressed every day. It might seem a little far-fetched to imagine your closet looking anything like a little boutique right now, but why not at least start dreaming about ways to treat yourself to a little more luxury by creating an environment that feels more pleasant to you at home? Dreaming can give us hope and inspiration to make things happen.

Luxury can be found in just *doing* little things for yourself every day to bring more comfort to your life at home. Even remembering simple routine tasks, such as opening up the curtains to let the light in instead of hanging out in your house all morning with the blinds down! Try opening your shades first thing in the morning and see how much better you feel.

Do It Now

Give yourself the luxury of a period of silence each day to focus only on YOU! Turn your phone off and indulge in something special. A bubble bath? Reading a book? A creative project? Even if it is just two minutes alone to shut your eyes, indulge in it without your phone or people or projects to distract you.

My daughter and her college roommates had a lovely ritual that inspired them to clean up their shared house and enjoy the process. (Yes, even college kids can create a little luxury for themselves and keep a tidy house.) Here's what they did to bring a bit of luxury to housekeeping: They lit a favorite candle, cracked the windows for a bit of fresh air, turned on some fancy music, such as Billie Holiday, and tidied up the house, refreshing it back to a lovelier state. The music and the candles made the cleaning experience feel so much more enjoyable. They created a sense of luxury without a lot of money or adding material items simply by turning on music and enjoying a nice scent while they cleaned.

There's a difference between just going through the motions of a day or coming to each experience as an opportunity to treat yourself a little more kindly. When you are aware of what extra details turn something into an enjoyable experience for you, suddenly spending time dusting your baseboards or mopping the floor feels like a more luxurious time because you decided it would be.

So often we forget to treat ourselves with the same level of hospitality that we would give to a guest. When you go to a nice hotel, you expect a certain atmosphere when you walk through the door. You expect the bed to be made and to find a neat little row of hotel toiletries lined up on the counter. We would be uncomfortable if we walked in and found clutter all over the bed and nightstand.

Why do we not consider these thoughtful luxuries more in our own homes? Yes, we do have to live there, so expecting it to be as perfect as a hotel might not be realistic in every way. But what about the ways we can take better care of the home we have? It's where we spend the most amount of our time. Perhaps we blame our lack of care for ourselves on finances, busyness, family, work, or the feeling that maybe we don't really deserve to have luxury in this season of our life, but we should find ways to take care of ourselves and offer little luxuries no matter what season of life we are in.

Love It

Feel pampered in your bathroom. Whether you take baths or showers, find an assortment of luxuries to indulge in when you need an evening to get away from it all. Find a special long-handled brush for washing your back, a hand massager for your neck, a luxurious soap or liquid gel, a beautiful, fluffy clean towel reserved only for you. (Have it monogrammed if you really want to be fancy!) Put out a pretty robe or pajamas and slippers for when you come out.

When I design areas of my home, I'm always thinking in terms of creating little corners I want to savor. Even if the tasks that have to be done in that space aren't all that enjoyable, the spot can be as delightful as a mini vacation.

How can I get the maximum enjoyment from even a small space? What activities do you dread? Let's say you have to pay bills. Who likes to pay bills? Not me. But if you are going to pay bills, you might as well set a luxurious scene in which to deplete your bank account. (Fortunately, you don't have to spend money to make your space feel luxurious.)

In a corner of a room, I might pull up a comfortable chair to a table. Maybe I will run around and find a little footstool to keep my legs from dangling and swinging with no place to land (short people problems). I'll add some luxurious accessories, such as a soft and fluffy throw blanket to keep me warm on a chilly evening of bill paying. If I will be paying bills with my laptop, I'll get my headphones so I can listen to music to make the experience even more pleasant. I'll do whatever I can think of to help set the ambience of that space so it is as comfortable and luxurious as I can make it.

Does that ambience seem overkill for bill paying? It shouldn't. It's an experience you have to have on a regular basis. Savoring your life and home is about setting the scene to make everyday activities more enjoyable.

Obviously, if I'm creating a luxurious little corner to savor, it really should not have clutter within view. Why do we live with clutter when it is so unsettling to us? Luxury and clutter don't belong in the same room. If you have excessive amounts of random clutter all over a room or even the entire house, you are going to feel stressed out. And living in stress doesn't feel like you are living in luxury! Now, here's a little unconventional advice. I'm sure most organizing experts would have a fit for what I am going to recommend. Even I am cringing just a little bit, but once I explain it I think you will understand why I believe this method can work if it's handled decisively.

If I am sick and tired of clutter everywhere and desperately need a tidy room, I will grab all of the clutter and take it somewhere else in the house and set up a designated clutter zone. Now, here's the deal on that idea. If at all possible, you should take the time then and there to put things in their home and not create a new zone for clutter. Don't make more work for yourself if you can save a step.

But if you have a room that is just too crazy to deal with in a short period of time, you might desperately want sanity in that space. Don't keep punishing yourself by living with the boxes of clutter stacked around the room. So here is how to solve that: Make the decision to pick just one other area for the clutter to hang out. Decide that you will not let it stay there forever, and put the date on your calendar for when you'll start dealing with it.

That might mean your garage is out of control for a while. Or an unused bedroom is filled to the brim. But here's why I am okay with a departure from the rules on occasion. Having clutter everywhere makes it impossible to find or savor even one sane spot. And if you cannot savor even one corner of your house, it's depressing. Why put yourself through that? Clutter moved to only one room really isn't any worse than leaving clutter spread all over the house. I just consider it containing the chaos.

Yes, ideally you'll declutter and remove excess from the house rather than rearranging where clutter hangs out. Clutter hidden in a bedroom is still there, so it hasn't truly solved your problem. But sometimes you need to have an empty room or closet in order to feel in control of one space. Your sanity is worth it.

Yet you should only trust yourself to get away with this method once you've committed to making better decisions and being more decisive. Now that you are working on being more deliberate, I have confidence you will also make the decision to not just leave that room forever in a state of chaos.

> *Making a decision to live clutter-free in one area,*
> *one room, or an entire floor of your house gives you*
> *the chance to start savoring your new way of living*
> *even if you haven't made it all the way around*
> *the house with your decluttering mission.*
> *That sounds luxurious to me!*
> *You deserve to have spaces that inspire you.*

Set up your home so you can feel taken care of and appreciated there. Even if you feel that no one else appreciates you, you should appreciate you!

Do the Things

Do you ever feel that you have spent a good part of your life collecting things to do the things you want to do, but then you don't do the things? You know what I'm talking about. You dream of scrapbooking, so you buy albums and fun little cutting tools, but you never make time to do it. You have pretty candles, but you never light them. You bought an elliptical machine to get in shape, but after the first day, you didn't find time to make it a part of your routine. My son will never let me forget that I bought a Wii Fit. It happens.

Make room in your life to do the things and use the things. Luxury doesn't necessitate new things at all. Luxury is about the experiences you create for yourself and your family to enjoy and then making it a priority to have those experiences.

When life gets filled with clutter and mess, or you are simply trying to keep up with your to-do list, it's easy to feel that you just don't have time for something that is luxurious. How could you make room for a daily indulgence, such as writing or playing an instrument? There will never be the perfect time for it; you just have to make the time for what you love. Perhaps you feel that you should be cleaning, not taking time for relaxing bubble baths! But you deserve that bubble bath. What is the point of having the tub or buying bubbles if you're always saving them for the perfect occasion?

You don't have to do all the things, but make the things you do memorable and enjoyable. Do more with less!

Love It

Hang a string of lights across your porch and plug them in every evening so you can see them sparkle from your kitchen.

Treat your family to luxury. No, you don't have to pack up and head to the islands for time together. Memories, even the simple ones, are the most luxurious gift you can give someone you love.

If you dream of family game nights around a real board game, stop dreaming and clear out that closet in your house of the junk and set aside an organized shelf for favorite family games. You'll be much more inspired to play them when they're easily accessible.

You might live with guilt that all the family photos you have are still on your phone. Treat your family to memories saved in special albums. Set yourself an alarm on your phone every day for a ten-minute break to tackle a part of the project to make you feel more organized. Keep a list of things to do with your ten minutes, such as sending photos off to be printed, adding a few photos to the scrapbook, or journaling.

Sit at the table together and ask everyone what the best and worst moment of their day was.

Go for a walk after dinner and look for treasures, such as pretty leaves and rocks.

Delight in Details

Luxury is found in the details of how we live and set up our home. We can embrace and create moments of delight in our day by finding small ways to surprise ourselves with joy.

I have a friend who had a set of battery-operated candles placed around the rooms in her house and in lanterns outside her front door. She set their built-in timer to turn them on automatically around the time she arrived home from work. What a lovely sight to come home to! She prepared the way to feel welcomed home. Doesn't that sound luxurious? It didn't take her much time or effort to treat herself to that nightly experience.

For years I had a secret little dream of having organized craft drawers. It seemed like something that would never actually happen. Who has time to get that organized anyway? My craft supplies were such a disaster. But because I decided I was going to make time and progress on these small indulgences as a gift to myself, I finally set up craft drawers that are organized and pretty to look at. It's as if a dream came true every time I open a drawer.

My secret for organized craft drawers is to use a shallow drawer system. I found mine at IKEA. The shallow drawers make organization a breeze because they don't allow for excess, and nothing gets lost as it might in a deep drawer.

Little details, such as lining drawers in pretty paper, may sound like a silly luxury when we have too much clutter to even see the paper lining the drawer. But when we get rid of the things we don't need and organize what we keep, we find we are effortlessly able to indulge in little details such as happy drawers.

There are lots of ways you can bring more luxury to your life even on a budget. You might decide what to save and what to splurge on in order to bring a little more luxury to an everyday experience. Focus on experiences and visual delights!

Love It

Set a pretty bound book with blank pages by your bed for dreaming and to keep track of lovely ideas for your life. Jot down new ideas to make your home more special.

Luxury is often perceived by the senses in the way we present something. How could you elevate the ordinary, everyday things you have? Once you declutter an area, give yourself a gift and fancy it up in some way without added clutter. As you go about your day cleaning and tidying, make the ordinary necessities seem like luxuries. Corral or hang things in a more attractive way.

Finish tidying up your home every day with your own flair for luxury! What else could you do to make your rooms feel special?

Ideas to
Elevate the Everyday

- Put pretty pens in a cute cup on your counter.

- Hang kids' art up on a doorway.

- Place a marble lazy Susan or a marble cutting board on your counter.

- Add a throw in a luxurious fabric, such as velvet, cashmere, faux fur, or knit.

- Line drawers with patterned paper.

- Find a cute little trinket dish for rings.

- Set up a coffee station with organized coffee supplies.

- Set up a "happy drawer" with unexpected delights.

- Put a crock by the stove filled with favorite utensils.

- Spritz your sheets with a natural essential oils scent.

- Add a fresh welcome mat at your entry.

- Put a seasonal wreath on the door.

- Put up strings of lights strung around the house, in a terrarium, or under a cloche for a pretty glow.

- Turn on lamps for yourself in the evening.

- Set the table with real place settings and sit at the table.
- Light candlesticks for a centerpiece, as if you are dining in a luxurious restaurant.
- Frame an uplifting quote and put it on a wall.
- Set a bouquet of flowers or greenery on the table.
- Put a bowl of fruit on your counter.
- Group favorite pitchers on an open shelf.
- Line up pretty cups in a cabinet.
- Include beautiful sounds to your home (music, wind chimes, a fountain).
- Have a kettle on the stove ready to make tea.
- Set up pretty binders lined up with labeled spines.
- Have pretty socks in a drawer, matched up and ready to choose from.
- Prepare fluffy, folded towels for the bath.
- Put dog food in a decorative tin can rather than leaving it in the bag (everyday on display).
- Put TV remotes on a tray on the coffee table.
- Add a stack of coasters for drinks.
- Set makeup brushes so they are standing up in a jar.

Pause, Reflect, and Act

Make Room

A home can feel like a hectic space. We have so much going on and so many things around that can keep it feeling cluttered and busy. How could you reclaim your home to feel more like an inviting retreat you want to come home to rather than a place you want to head away from? What frugal luxuries do you need to make room for in your home?

Let it Go

Do you have necessities you keep around your house that aren't enjoyable to use? For example, do you have old hand soaps or worn sheets? Does your bedroom feel more like a storage locker than a luxurious, inviting place to rest and spend time with your spouse? Let go of what is no longer inspiring and replace what you can with a fresher, more luxurious option.

Home Love Habit

As you go through each day, begin to pay closer attention to the state of your home. Observe practical items you use regularly that you do not find beautiful. How could you pare down to fewer items that will bring more enjoyment in their use? Start a habit of regularly decluttering down to simple luxuries rather than hoarding many things you don't love.

10

Unpack Your Story

*The ability to simplify means to eliminate the unnecessary
so that the necessary may speak.*

HANS HOFMANN

I f what you are passionate about inspires your home, your home
will in turn inspire you to live more fully and gracefully every day.
Creating a home is a worthy adventure, but it takes time. A home
cannot be rushed to completion. To truly reflect those who live there,
it will always be evolving. The joy is in the journey, so it will take time
to tell the story as you live it chapter by chapter. Be patient with yourself and have fun along the way. No detail or effort is wasted when it's
incorporated with love into your home.

Reflecting your heart and life in the design and organization of your
home isn't always an easy thing to pull off with style. There is a fine line
between showing off what you love through personal collections in your
home and trinkets that end up looking overly cluttered or even tacky
because they don't reflect your style today. Paying attention to those
finer details of how to reflect your story make a home feel truly inspired.

As you consider designing and organizing your home for the people who live there, you'll want to incorporate details that really matter
to them. Whether it's how the home is organized or styled, you want
to reflect and make room for the people first and foremost. We should

design our life first and then incorporate into our home the ideas and function that will inspire that life.

A house staged for a magazine cover may look beautiful on the newsstands, but it won't necessarily feel quite like *home* in real, every-day life if it doesn't reflect the people who inhabit it or how they live.

How you display and incorporate what you love will feel more authentic when it is naturally displayed and makes sense for the peo-ple in your family. Create a sanctuary, not a showplace! Blankets that are styled by draping them dramatically from chairs down to the floor ready to trip people as they walk by, accessories teetering so precari-ously on a side table that if anyone looks at them closely a calamity will likely result, or organizational systems that are pretty but don't allow your entire family to use them with ease are details that don't make sense in a home for a family.

A truly beautiful home always begins with authenticity. It should be beautiful not just because it's designed in a pretty or stylish way, but because the choices and decisions make sense when you get to know the people who live there.

*An authentic home always tells a story, so make sure
yours is telling the story you want to be told.*

Whether you just recently moved in or have lived in your home for years, it's time to nestle in and learn to fully live in every room of your house. Unpack all the boxes (raise your hand if you still have areas of your home that you haven't unpacked and you've lived there longer than a year!). How will your home tell your story? Go ahead. Look at your home in a new way, rearrange the furniture, and get settled in.

Let Go of Things You Loved

As you go through your house trying to make sense of what you have acquired and saved (finding so many random things in boxes and asking yourself, *Why, oh why did we save that?*) you'll undoubtedly come across things that reflect little snapshots of your life and who you were and what you loved at a moment in time.

My daughter Courtney and I spent several years working together on a decluttering mission, going through every closet, every box, and every room all through the house to declutter, organize, and beautify each space.

I went on a year-long epic paper-decluttering mission, and piece by piece I watched our entire life flash before us in paper. Virtually every single piece of paper I had saved all those years? Completely unnecessary. I never needed any of it. I never even looked through the boxes. I never would have been able to find anything even if I'd needed to! It was all too much. Yet I carted those boxes of papers through each move to every new house, just in case. I filled up closets with file boxes of paper and garage shelves with random totes of files. Paper was not my friend.

So I bought a giant paper shredder and shredded every bit of it. I shredded the contents of boxes filled with old receipts, bills, school papers, notes, credit cards, statements, and jumbled up papers of the most random stuff representing years of our life and things we had loved and lived through. Good memories and not-so-good memories. You name it, I shredded it! If it was important or special enough that I needed or wanted to hang on to it (which was really very little), I set up files for what I needed so I could find it.

We made more space for what we loved in each and every room. Each box of paper we shredded, each item we decluttered or gave away, opened up more room. It was getting addictive to declutter, and we began to thrive on establishing order for what remained. What a joy to open a drawer and see only what we loved!

The linen closet, the office, the kitchen, the bedrooms, the family room, the bathrooms...we went through each one! We even went through the garage, something we had put off for so long. So much decluttering, so much reorganizing of what was left. What a project! Everything wasn't perfect in our home and still isn't, but everything was so much better than it was before.

I'll admit, though, that occasionally I had a really hard time letting go of things. Sometimes it was because I loved it, even though I didn't need it. Other times it was because I believed I would use it for a better purpose later if I just hung on to it.

Do It Now

Look around your house. What has been hanging on your walls or sitting on tables or in cabinets forever? Ask yourself to tell the story of that item. If it doesn't have a good story that means something to you, let it go!

At one point I was decluttering a dish cabinet because I was starting to feel overwhelmed by the excessive amount of platters and bowls stored in it. They were stacked so high that it was frustrating to pull any of them out, so I dreaded using them. But I kept hanging on to them in spite of how overly stuffed my cabinet was. Every time I thought about getting rid of some of those things, I pictured how cool it would be to have extras so I would be able to take treats to people and give them a cute platter too! Such a lovely and generous daydream, but I didn't actually follow through on it often enough to make a dent.

Well, soon it dawned on me that to keep so much that I didn't need or to use for some future time when I would be more generous was a bit selfish. Why not be generous now? I had friends at church who loved the platters, so I cleaned out the cabinet and brought them for the ladies to choose from one Sunday. What a joy it was to see how happy these ladies were to bring a platter home! Yeah, it would have been awesome had I baked treats and handed them out on the platters. But because finding time to bake treats was the one thing that had prevented me from giving them away before, it wasn't worth waiting for that perfect scenario to be generous.

We were thrilled to no longer be slaves to clutter and indecision, and our home felt cleaner and more organized than it had ever been. Finally, there were only two spaces left to fully declutter. One was a walk-in closet we had avoided for years, and the other was the space under the house.

The year before we had pulled some frames and family photos out of the walk-in closet to design a family photo wall, something I had wanted to do ever since we moved in. Just seeing those memories up on our walls did my heart good. What good is it to keep things you love hidden away where they cannot be enjoyed?

When it came time to move out of our house, we finally had to face the rest of that closet. Fortunately, it wasn't space we necessarily needed for anything else over the years because we couldn't have added anything to it if we had tried. Our first instinct was to be ashamed of how much stuff we had in that closet. Why so much?

We had downsized when we moved in years before, and by the amount of stuff we crammed in that closet, it was pretty clear we had not downsized enough. Everything in it was as if it was frozen in time six years back to the day we moved in. We were so busy in that season, and going through so many changes at that time, that this closet wasn't a priority. So many random bits and pieces of our story, special photos, and memories were left there as we moved on with life.

While we were ashamed that we had so much stuff in there, we also realized what this space symbolized. While it was filled with many things we loved and we still had to face what to do with it all, it was also a reminder that we were finally near the end of our massive decluttering mission, and we were coming to the end of dealing with leftover decisions from our old ways. We've learned so many new habits since the day we put all of that stuff in there.

We no longer let indecision or disorganization take over, at least for long, so this space was truly a time capsule of how things were. It felt victorious to realize that while we still had to go through so much stuff in that closet and under the house, we had gained new habits for how to deal with it and felt confident for how we could be stronger to resist that level of indecision or disorganization in the future.

Each time we downsize or declutter, we must let go of more things—even things we love. Decluttering is messy business. We don't want to open up that closet door or dig around in the basement because it's a reminder of our past, our disorganization, our indecisiveness. We can't deal with the past if we aren't ready to be more decisive, and sometimes we just don't feel ready to make those decisions.

Not only do we have to drag things out of dark corners and boxes and make big messes to sort through things we haven't looked at in years, we have to sometimes face good or painful memories, make decisions we've put off for a very long time, and sometimes even say goodbye to things from chapters of our life because they are no longer serving us. It's messy, but so worth it to live more fully right now.

Saying goodbye to the past and reforming your old habits isn't easy. You have to enter right into the mess, bring it all out into the open, and own it. Every last piece of it. Each piece of paper, every trinket, all the little objects and random things you've held on to for years. The clutter, the stuff, indecision—don't let any of it stand between you and what you envision for your life or your home.

Don't fear the mess. Fear the result of keeping it.

Peter Walsh, an organizational expert, describes clutter as being one of two general types. "Memory clutter" is stuff that reminds us of special events in our life, such as ticket stubs and travel brochures. "Someday clutter" refers to things you don't want to let go of because you think you may use them someday. If you give that bowl away, what if you need it next Thanksgiving?

Clutter all comes down to the hesitation you have in letting things go, doesn't it? When you own your stuff, you'll start to see those piles upon piles of stuff as a result of your indecision about how to handle past and present belongings. Owning your stuff and overcoming those old habits means you will commit to taking control of what in is your home right now and enjoy using it rather than letting stuff you hold on to from the past, or for the future to control your life right now.

We own our stuff when we use it! We own our stuff when we love it enough to make it a part of our life right now. If we own it, it takes a special place of honor in our life. Clutter just weighs us down and keeps us feeling stressed out rather than allowing us to enjoy what we have in the present.

Incorporate Your Story

Many years ago, I was quite intrigued by an article in *Traditional Home* magazine. Surprisingly, the featured home was inspired by a circus theme. Normally, themed rooms don't resonate with me, and besides, clowns are terrifying. I never would have imagined I could be drawn to a circus-themed house! Not many people can pull off a theme like that without it looking a little goofy. But these homeowners succeeded. Were they in the circus? No, but when I read the backstory on their life, their home made sense. It wasn't one bit scary.

You see, their home was originally headquarters to a well-known circus! Their address? One Circus Place. The architecture of their home was stunning, the circus influences through the decor were tasteful and subtle, and the cheery, bright, clear colors and fanciful furnishings overflowed with youthful exuberance. Each detail pulled together a winning combination of style that reflected the history of the home and the personal taste and life of the young family.

What does your home say about you? Does it reflect the story you want it to tell? When you decorate in a way that stirs your heart and soul, whether it is through colors and textures or furniture you love or bits and pieces of your life story, the connection you feel to your home will inspire you to embrace the joy in your life. With the right mementos from your past around you brought together in full acknowledgment of who you are today, you'll see each part of your home as a reminder to count your blessings every day. By inviting in things you love, you'll feel more deeply connected to your home in a way that will inspire your life.

Do you feel stuck in how to feel more connected to your home or incorporate more of what you love? Do you struggle with a home that is perhaps so cluttered or stuck in the past that you cannot imagine it being filled only with what is meaningful to you today?

Perhaps to fully embrace your style now, you acknowledge where you've been. What positive experiences influenced the person you are today? When we feel stuck about what to do with all those boxes in the attic or garage or the piles filling up our surfaces and closets, it helps to make sense of them in light of how we feel our past could be better honored in our present.

What are some of your happiest memories? What are you passionate about, and how did you begin to develop that part of your life? In what tangible ways could you incorporate where you came from into who you are today? What are some stories and special memories you want your family to remember? Are there even small but meaningful ways to pay tribute to your past by connecting them to your life right now?

Perhaps you'll be inspired to dig out some long-forgotten boxes from the attic to remember more clearly parts of your story you've forgotten or kept apart from your life. To be fully connected to our home, we need to unpack what is kept stagnant in storage so we can invite what is memorable to be part of our life.

Love It

Go through your memory boxes and dressers and find ticket stubs, postcards, letters and cards of memories of people and places you love. Arrange them on an inspiration board or frame a couple of things to hang on the wall to inspire you!

When we endeavor to feel connected to what we see around us, and make what we love part of our life, we will need to get tough as we go through those boxes in our house to decide what will stay and what will go.

Do you have boxes of stuff you say you love piled high in the attic? Boxes in the attic can't tell the full story. Do you have clutter jammed in the closet so tightly that you couldn't even find your treasures if you wanted to show them off? Not inspiring. Are trinkets overflowing every surface, making it nearly impossible to tell the story of what is treasured and what is not? Confusing.

That's the thing about stuff. Too much of it nullifies the enjoyment of anything. When it's packed away where you can't even see it, it isn't part of your life. To love it, it needs to be active in your life.

But what about all the stuff you feel that you should keep but don't know what to do with? What if you have too many things you love or things that have sentimental value to you or your family? You probably have things in your home you feel obligated to keep or have a hard time parting with. You know the stuff I'm talking about. The china you were given for your wedding that sits in a box in the garage because you don't have room for it. The letterman's jacket you were so proud of in 1989. The cat sculpture your favorite aunt made and wanted you to have before she passed away. The box of old letters and postcards from people you love.

It might seem simple to declutter in theory, but when we dig deep into those closets and attics, we find things that are not easy to let go of. We can better honor the space we have and incorporate it into our story when we are able to find joy in making sentimental things part of our life.

Seven Ideas for Unpacking and Making More Room for the Sentimental Things You Love

1. Show them off. Frame children's old artwork and display around the house, hang heirloom plates as dining room decor, make a family photo gallery wall. Shadow boxes can hold little trinkets and jewelry. Jars can hold all sorts of collections and memories, such as photos, shells, and small collectibles.

2. Share the love. Offer a sentimental item to another family member who would enjoy the memories just as much as you do but will have more room to display them. Give special treasures as holiday gifts to people who will love them. It's fun to give gifts that have a story.

3. Pare down. Keep one; lose the rest. One sentimental plate treasured and on display will be more meaningful than keeping the entire 12-piece set hidden away in a box.

4. Take a photo. Acknowledge and cherish the memories but lose the clutter. Photograph the item for an album if you want to be sure to remember it.

5. Repurpose. Make it into something functional so it's more useful. Turn your dad's old flannel shirt into a pillow you can enjoy every day!

Hang maps and postcards you've collected on a travel memory inspiration board for a wall.

6. *Make it more worthy.* Sell it and then donate the money to a cause you believe in so you feel good about your choice.

7. *Give generously.* Give items away, knowing that what you have been holding on to will now bring joy to others.

When you've lived fully (you've explored, created memories, loved, cried, laughed, and lived not just for yourself but for and with others), your home can be filled with beautiful reminders of what has mattered most to you. Unpack things and then give away or recycle what is simply clutter and live surrounded by what you love.

Make Room for Possibilities

There is much to be excited about in the hunting and gathering of what you love. Finding new things and the adventures by which they were acquired become wonderful parts of our story. If you are currently in a state of feeling overwhelmed by how much you've already gathered, remember back to how you used to feel before clutter took over. Do you remember the joy you used to find in the adventure of creating a home?

I remember my delight over each and every item my husband and I added to our home when we were newly married. We were given many things to set up our first house, but it was the treasures we discovered and chose together that always meant the most to us. We would stop at garage sales, scour estate sales, and browse gift shops during little trips we took together. We found such joy in finding things we loved, and those experiences where treasures were gathered became a part of our story.

We still love stopping in secondhand stores, art galleries, and estate sales to see what we might discover, but there was a season when we made an agreement to not do that anymore. No more stuff could come in. Our home was filled to the brim, stuffed to capacity, and we did not need a single new thing in it. While that was a wise pact during a season of life when we needed to declutter, we discovered that what we missed the most were the adventures we used to have together. It wasn't just about acquiring stuff, but the togetherness involved in the discovering.

Not to worry, not to fear. This is not an endless cycle of making room for more stuff. True contentment with what you have won't mean you will have to keep acquiring things until you have all the things you could ever want and then making room to get some more things. No, no, no. You will never be content in that endless cycle, nor will you find joy in staying stuck in a home that is fully stuffed. The goal is not to empty it so that you can fill it back up again with more stuff. The reason to make more room in your home is to make more room to fully *live*.

Decluttering all of the things we've held on to for so long isn't as scary as it might have seemed when we first began the process. When we hold firm to our resolve that we will no longer be held hostage by all the baggage and clutter we invited in, we make more room for what we love, for embracing life to the full, dreaming big dreams, and inviting in life's new exciting adventures! By letting things go that have tied us down and stood in our way, we will feel free.

Pause, Reflect, and Act

Make Room

Your home should have room to incorporate the story of who you are today and where you've come from. Tell your story through art, books, colors, textures, photos, and treasures. Unpack the boxes to find mementos you can use to tell the story!

Let It Go

Your story has wonderful chapters from the past that are worthy and wonderful to remember, but don't let your home get stuck in a time capsule. It's okay to let past trinkets go in order to make more room for what inspires you now. They served their purpose at that time. Now make more room for who you have become.

Home Love Habit

Make more room for what you love now by only keeping what is useful and beautiful to honor the space you have. Designing a home that inspires you can be a cherished part of your life, so make it a habit to continually refine what you keep and decisively let go of that which is no longer serving its purpose. Projects can be finished, but a home should be ever-evolving, just like you!

ORGANIZE & DECLUTTER

THE

MAKE
ROOM

CHALLENGE

Make Room for What Matters Most to You

Do you ever take a look at your house and just feel *overwhelmed*? Does it seem nearly impossible to make a noticeable dent in the mess? Do you feel paralyzed when you think about where to begin to restore order?

Do not fear. When you look at the overflowing mess in closets and cabinets and floors and beds and drawers and kitchens and bedrooms and bathrooms...it IS overwhelming. It's too much. I don't blame you if you ever wish that a giant donation or dump truck would come and take it all away.

A pile of clutter doesn't make anyone happy. The process of paring down to what you really love will ultimately lead to more freedom and less stress. Letting go of what you don't need right now will add so much more joy to your life than continuing the futile struggle to organize the excess. The *less* you hang on to, the *more* peace you will have.

As you've looked through the pages of this book, you've probably spent some time considering how simple changes in your own actions and attitudes could transform your space. Perhaps you've even started working on some areas of your home. If you are ready to be challenged to go further, to help facilitate the process in the following pages, I'm sharing what I call the Make Room Challenge, a simplified plan that offers distinct, action-oriented tasks for decluttering and organizing, centered around five activity zones in your home.

Make Room Challenge Overview

1. Make Room for Rest and Rejuvenation
   Focus: Master Bedroom

2. Make Room for Primping and Pampering
   Focus: Master Bathroom

3. Make Room for Arrivals and Departures
   Focus: Paper Clutter and Entry

4. Make Room for Playing and Creating
   Focus: Play and Creative Spaces

5. Make Room for Feasting and Gathering
   Focus: Kitchen and Gathering Spaces

Do these tasks at your own pace, but commit to being a finisher. You can repeat or refine many of these tasks as needed until you reach your goals. If you are further along on the journey, you can begin to beautify the space or improve your organizational systems or move on to additional rooms. The goal of these tasks is to inspire you to make progress in these key areas and to experience the joy of measurable results.

Each of these activity zones includes a power clean session so you can feel accomplished with the finished product and be inspired to move on to the next! As you spend time on these tasks, my hope is that you will not only find joy in the beautiful results of a less cluttered and tidier space, but that you will have more room in your schedule and home for everything, and everyone that matters in your life.

TIP: If you need organizing or space-saving supplies for your home, you can find many of our recommendations at makeroomforwhatyoulove.com.

Make Room for Rest and Rejuvenation

Retreating to your master bedroom should feel like a reward at the end of a long day. It's a sacred space. In a serene haven, clutter is an unwelcome housemate. In order to launch into your day with energy and anticipation, you need to have the areas where you keep clothes organized and functional, and your purse and wallet uncluttered so you can feel put together no matter what the next day might bring. Even if you have a lot to declutter or organize, the following missions are designed to inspire success over manageable bits of time.

FOCUS:
Master Bedroom

+ Closet
+ Dresser
+ Purse

Refine Your Closet Hanging Space

Getting dressed and looking put together make us feel as if we are ready for anything. But when our closet is in disarray, we feel like a disaster. Let's reset our closets so they can be more useful and inspiring.

1. Take everything hanging in your closet out and lay it across the bed. Also pick up anything that should be hanging in your closet but is lying out on furniture, the floor, or elsewhere in the house. If you have a lot of laundry to do, set aside some time to catch up before you move on to the next step

2. Make a visual note of how much space you have for your hanging items. That's your everyday hanging space, so you are only going to use it for in-season clothes you actually wear regularly. If you don't have anyplace else to hang

clothes that are for another season or specialty items, you'll need to leave room in the closet for those items too.

3. Item by item, pick up from the bed what you would wear this week or in the next few weeks. Focus on this season only and on items that fit well and are in good condition.

4. Assess whether you actually need so many similar pieces, or if several complete outfits made from classics and basics mixed with a few fun accessories would serve you better than dozens of random or lone items. Consider how many and what types of clothes you can actually wear given your weekly schedule. You might only need one little black dress rather than five, three trendy blouses rather than ten, and two pairs of nice jeans rather than seven.

5. Put your clothes back in your closet, from longest to shortest, category by category, left to right: hang the dresses, the pants, skirts, and followed by the longer sweaters or jackets, then the shirts.

6. If you have hanging accessories, such as belts, hang them on a belt hanger or looped through a regular hanger on the left side of the closet if there's room. Set aside your scarves and other accessories to tackle in another project.

7. If the closet is stuffed again, pare down some more. See if anything that was hanging could be folded (jeans or T-shirts) or hung elsewhere if you really do wear it often.

8. Your hanging space should be easy to get into and to find what you are looking for. Step back and admire how efficient and pretty your hanging space looks now!

9. Look back at what is left on the bed. What would you wear it right now if it was a different season or a special occasion (and only consider what fits right now)? If you have no other closet for your out-of-season or specialty clothes, put those items in this closet too (according to

their length). If the closet gets too stuffed again, you'll have to pare down.

10. Whatever is left can be donated! Take the clothes out to the car and drop them off. You'll make someone's day, and you'll be really happy in the morning when you can get dressed without wrestling with hangers.

Get Organized Tips

- Invest in matching hangers! Now that you've pared down your wardrobe to what will comfortably fit in your closet, count how many hangers you need and only buy that amount (don't get extras). Your closet will look tidier if the hangers are the same or at least the same color. Buy slim, nonslip hangers whenever possible.

- If your closet rod is still a little too stuffed but you aren't sure what else should go yet, here's a tried-and-true tip: Hang all of your hangers backwards. Every time you wear an item, put it back into the closet with the hanger facing forward. Whatever hanging is still facing backward after a month is not worn often enough to take up your valuable real estate!

Tidy Your Closet Shelves, Floor, and Shoe Area

Now that your hanging space is looking so good and so much more functional, let's get the rest of your closet decluttered.

1. Grab everything off the closet floor and shelves and toss it out into the room.

2. Get all the shoes out.

3. Dust the shelves and vacuum or sweep the floors.

4. Look at the space you have available on shelves or any shoe organizers. That's your everyday space. It is not endless and does not grow as we stuff more into it, so let's make it more functional and easy to use.

5. What needs to go on the shelves? What should actually be hanging? Pare as needed to make room for what belongs on the rod.

6. Look through the items you have to put back and select only what you will realistically wear this week or in the next few weeks. If it's in poor condition, doesn't fit, or you avoid wearing it, don't put it back in the closet.

7. Make the shelves functional (decide how many items you can stack without a hassle to get them out) and fold the items carefully so they look tidy. Group purses, shoes, sweaters, and T-shirts.

8. Shoes can be tucked into back-of-the-door or wall shoe pockets, an extra drawer, or an under-the-bed organizer for easy access if you don't have room in your closet. Make a list of future organizers or supplies you need to make the most of the space you have.

Declutter Your Dresser

If you have a dresser or drawers in a closet or other storage pieces, take a moment to pare down and tidy things up.

1. Empty your clothing and belongings from dresser drawers.

2. Take advantage of this moment to wipe them out and even add new drawer liners if you want to.

3. Take stock of how much drawer space you have. What do you need your drawer space for? Assign each drawer a purpose, with space for each category of belongings (such as socks, undies, slips, tights, pjs.).

4. Now it's time to put back what you really use. What is in good condition, fits, and you actually like to wear? Put those items back in the drawer in the designated space. Match up socks. If you have lone socks, start a lonely sock basket, and if the mate turns up you'll be able to return them to the dresser. If the drawers become too crowded, pare down or relocate items if you have another option.

5. What's left? It's time to donate or dispose. Take the rest out immediately to finish the task!

6. Return to wipe off the dresser top and make it pretty.

Get Organized Tips

You can make easy DIY drawer dividers from old shoe and gift boxes.

Just can't decide what to keep or let go of yet? Have an undecided box. Put things in there that are still under consideration, but commit to yourself that you have to make a decision by the end of the month. At the end of the month, if you haven't made a decision, let things go!

Power Clean

Set aside a longer block of time to clean one bedroom today top to bottom.

Put on your cleaning outfit, turn the playlist on, crack a window, light a nice candle, and visualize how wonderful it will be to have a clean room!

- Wash sheets, pillowcases, blankets.
- Clear off nightstands and tidy them up.

- Remove clutter from floors.
- Vacuum carpet or rugs, or sweep and dust hardwood floors.
- Clean out under the bed.
- Dust all surfaces, baseboards, lampshades, and window sills.
- Polish up accessories and lamps.
- Put away clean laundry.
- Make bed with clean sheets.
- Fluff and line up pillows.
- Fold a throw blanket at end of bed as a finishing touch!

Future Bonus Points Now that you have organized your clothing items in your available space, have some fun combining complete outfits. Make sure you have the top, the bottom, the shoes, the camisole, the belt, the jacket, the jewelry. Take photos of options and save them in your phone or on a bulletin board in the closet. This process will make it easier for you to be creative mixing and matching what you already have. Outfit organization will also make it more clear what you might need to add or remove from your wardrobe!

Once you are happy with your personal spaces for rest and rejuvenation, you can go through other bedrooms and closets in your house and refine them to suit the people in those spaces.

CELEBRATE! Curl up with a good book and a cup of tea and delight in how wonderful it feels to have such a pretty and organized room. Sleep tight!

Make Room for Primping and Pampering

FOCUS:
Master Bathroom

+ Makeup
+ Hair
+ Nails
+ Bathing
+ Jewelry
+ Accessories

Now that you're able to effortlessly get into your closet and dresser to find clothes to wear, the next step is to get organized so you can add the finishing flourishes to your look before you face the day. This zone takes place around the master bathroom or wherever you keep and use your personal beauty and styling supplies.

Now, I'm sure you are naturally just lovely in the morning even without a little mascara. And even if you stay at home to work or have the privilege of chasing after tiny humans all day and jewelry feels a bit frivolous, little details of self-care matter more than you might think! Not only will you notice a change in the way you carry yourself and your attitudes about the day, but the positive effect of YOU feeling more pulled together can be a domino toward you feeling more inspired to pull your home together too.

Simplify Bathroom Essentials

1. Pare down towels to only your best of the best (perhaps to simplify, set a goal of just two bath towels per person, two hand towels, and several washcloths.) Make a note to invest in a new set if your towels look like they've seen better days.

2. Pare down any necessary cleaning products in this space to just one or two all-purpose cleaners.

3. Clean out the medicine cabinet and safely discard old products and medications.

Set Up Your Beauty Station

Let's declutter the unused cosmetics and beauty products and then get organized!

1. Empty the drawers or any storage containers in the bathroom. Throw away any facial products you don't use or are expired. Weed out old or never-used nail polish too! Check each bottle of polish to see if you can open it successfully.

2. Set aside makeup items you don't use regularly but you think you are likely to use on a certain occasion (fancy lipstick or eye shadow, for instance). Put those items in a separate pouch or box.

3. Pare down hair accessories, styling tools, and products to only what you use and love. Look in the shower or tub area and declutter all the excess.

4. Set aside jewelry. We'll organize that separately.

5. Group together styling and pampering items by category (hair, face, nails, body, teeth).

6. Next, gather appropriate organizers and containers. (Use what you have to get started. Look around the house for small boxes, saucers, pouches, cosmetic bags, or small bowls. You can always fancy things up later!)

7. Place your bag or box of rarely used items in a less convenient or visible location.

8. Set up an area, drawer, or basket for each category so everything you need regularly has a home that is convenient and organized.

- If you have double sinks with space in between on the counter and need more storage space, add a cute basket to stash your hairbrushes or cosmetics, jars for makeup brushes, attractive bottles for bubble bath, or a tiered shelving unit to hold towels or extra supplies. Group things that have to stay visible into cute containers, baskets, or jars.

- Use the space under the sinks by adding plastic drawers, small shelves, or dollar store plastic containers to organize and label items in categories (such as nail polish products or hair products).

Organize Your Accessories Station

Owning and organizing versatile accessories can creatively expand your wardrobe options, allowing you to mix up your look without overstuffing your closet. Let's dive into creating an accessible and organized place to create more style in less space!

1. Find all of your scarves, jewelry, and accessories and bring them into one location near your clothing. Start with the scarves, and pick out any you like to wear regularly (unless you already organized scarves on a shelf on a previous day!). Do you have hooks, a scarf hanger, basket, or a shelf for scarves? Hang hooks or set up a basket to organize the scarves you want to be able to wear.

2. Group jewelry by what you want to wear and really like. Then divide the items you use into groups of earrings, rings, bracelets, and necklaces.

3. Set up a simple system and a home for each. The

important thing is to have jewelry accessible and ready to use right away, so there's no need to go shopping or get fancy with organizers (at least yet). To simplify for now so you can move forward, necklaces can be hung on the wall or on a bulletin board with pushpins or hooks. Hang earrings from a ribbon on a wall or on a corkboard. Bracelets can go on hooks, on a plate, on a tray, or in a basket.

Now when you feel as if you have nothing to wear, you can head to your Accessories Station instead of the shopping mall, so pat yourself on the back for a job well done!

Get Organized Tips

- Do you have hooks on the back of your doors and on the wall? If not, make a note to add them so you can easily hang a towel, robe, purse, or even your outfit for the day to keep everything off the floor.

- Where do you get dressed? Place a laundry hamper in that space.

- Put a small tray, basket, or shelf near the toilet to hold extra TP, a candle, or air freshener.

- Organize perfumes on a tray if you like to wear fragrances.

- Add a plant to purify the air and to bring a little life to your space.

- How could you refine your organizing system in the future to be even more attractive or better suited for your belongings?

- What special touches could you add to your bathroom to make it better reflect your style?

Prepare Your Purse

A tidy purse and decluttered wallet will make you feel polished and organized for the day's errands. No one relishes that awkward moment of fishing a wallet out from under all the receipts at the bottom of a disorganized purse. Especially that grand moment (just after you've spent 90 embarrassing seconds trying to catch flying receipts from that incident) when you begin removing a wad of gum that has affixed itself to the outside of the wallet (who among us has not done that?). Let's restore our dignity and become the more graceful and poised woman we dream of being.

1. Clear out your purse completely, including your wallet, empting all pockets and compartments.

2. Recycle wrappers and trash and put away all necessary receipts and papers.

3. Put essential cash, debit or credit cards, and health cards back into your wallet.

4. Add small, zippered pouches to corral loose items for better organization (makeup, reward cards, coins, personal items, or for temporarily storing receipts).

5. Designate a particular pocket to keep your cell phone and keys, so you can easily grab them when needed.

6. Create your own little purse-sized emergency kit so you're prepared for anything (a small kit of first aid supplies, such as Band-Aids, pain medication, toiletries, laundry pen, mints, cash).

Power Clean

Set aside a longer block of time to give your bathroom a thorough cleaning. If you really want to pamper yourself, there's no guilt or shame in hiring a professional housekeeper to do the job or part of this job for you, especially if it has been a while since it has been cleaned. (I hired someone to clean my shower when I was preparing to move, and it was a GAME CHANGER. I had no idea the glass doors of my shower could be so sparkly clean!) Even if you just need help the first time and then maintain it yourself going forward, it might be a worthwhile splurge.

But not to worry! You can totally do this yourself. Get yourself ready by putting your cleaning outfit on, grabbing the tunes and your supplies, and let's get this party started!

- Take down and wash the shower curtain, liner, and any window curtains. If you have blinds instead, clean them.
- Start at the top and wipe down window molding, sills, shelves, walls, light fixtures, and cabinet faces.
- Clean the mirrors.
- Clean out the drawers if they haven't been wiped out recently.
- Clean the toilet bowl and polish the top, sides, and toilet base (and the floor around it).
- With a clean rag, clean the tub or shower.
- Polish the counter and sinks and counter accessories.
- Sweep floors and mop.
- Rehang the curtains and shower curtains.

Future Bonus Points If you are inspired to go through this mission again, make your way through other bathrooms to declutter, organize, tidy, and beautify.

CELEBRATE! I think this calls for a bubble bath. Or even just locking yourself in the bathroom with the music up and the water running so you can experience a few moments of peace in your clean and tidy bathroom.

Make Room for Arrivals and Departures

The arrival and departure areas of our home tend to collect quite a bit of clutter and often end up in disarray. We bring in a lot of papers, coats, schoolbags, purses, briefcases, sports equipment, homework, party invitations, and bills, and we track in mud and grime from outside. How do those clutter spots make you feel when they are out of control?

FOCUS:
Paper Clutter
and Entry

+ Paper
+ Entry

Chances are these items contribute to the less-than-graceful moments that stress us out every day both in and outside the home. Let's tackle some of these clutter magnets and beautify the functional spaces that surround our areas of arrival and departure. The goal is progress, not perfection. Each time you go through this process of challenging yourself to focus on a space, you'll make even more progress.

Set Up a Simple Yearly Filing System

The secret to controlling paper clutter is having a plan for it as soon as it enters the house. Get a file box or use a file drawer to set up a simple filing system for papers you may need to access in the current year. Label a folder for each category, such as tax documents, insurance documents, medical records, home, car, loan documents, important receipts, and warranties. Don't make your filing system too complicated to start out. Only keep on hand what is essential in the current year. Papers you need to save longer term (such as tax documents) can be moved to a separate filing system.

You can use a scanner to store files when you are not required to keep an original document, but it may be more efficient to start with a paper file system first. Paper files are simple to use and affordable. You can always graduate to a scanner when you are ready to invest in and tackle a new system.

Set Up a Family Command Center

Whether you have bills, party invitations, school calendars, or other reminders in your home, you'll want a system for what to do with papers you need to take action on. Electronic calendars, bill paying services, and phone reminders can eliminate paper clutter and keep you alerted to activities. Take some time to set those systems up if you feel they would be beneficial to your family.

However, if you prefer paper you can set up a centralized command center in your home to keep your family organized with the current papers, calendars, invitations, to-do lists, and schedules of the family and school. It can be a cork bulletin board, a magnetic whiteboard, or even clipboards affixed to the wall. The command center should only be used for urgent items that have a deadline. Put it in a central location where you'll pass it often, such as the entry or kitchen, and get in the habit of clearing out old papers weekly. Bills to pay should have their own distinct destination, such as a basket, file, or special clip on your command center.

Set Up a Paper Sorting Station

The main mistake in handling paper pileups begins at the door. Avert the crisis by knowing exactly where to go with each piece of paper.

1. Find a spot near your entry or office area (or your command center) where you'll take all incoming mail.

2. Put a shredder and recycling bin near this station so you'll be able to immediately deal with papers you don't want.

3. Plan to sort, shred, or recycle all the envelopes, newspapers, and junk mail and put your bills in your previously designated spot every time you bring the mail in the house.

4. Everything that is not a bill but has a due date or an

upcoming deadline can go on your command center board with a clip or pin.

5. If a paper is important and you'll need to access it later, file it in your designated file box or drawer.

6. Give each housemate an inbox if they will receive mail or have papers that enter the house.

7. If your child comes home with special papers you want to keep, get a clear box with a lid or a personal file box with folders to store the current year report cards, favorite assignments, art, and other significant papers.

Deal with Past Paper Pileups

Bring all of your piled papers together in one room. If you have closets and drawers full of papers, empty each one and bring all of the paper into a room near a shredder and recycling bin. Yes, that may feel overwhelming, but you'll be empowered to succeed when you see how many papers have been stuffed in hiding. Your closets and drawers will feel open and decluttered, inspiring you to never let paper clutter pile up again. Your paper clutter will only be in one room, encouraging you to make and see progress. Tackle sorting one pile at a time! You can also call a paper recycler to pick up (or you can drop off) boxes of papers to avoid the need for you to shred each item individually.

Power Clean

Today's the day to declutter and refresh the area just inside your door—the entry space you first see as you enter your home.

1. Assess your entry. Whether it is big or basically just drops you right into the living room, there is space around the door to enter. Is it inspiring and functional?

2. Do you have a coat closet? Pare down what is in it (try for 50 percent less) so you can use it to a greater potential. Don't worry about making it perfect at this point. Just

remove some excess to give it room to breathe. You can come back and declutter and organize it some more down the road.

3. Declutter the entry.

4. Shake out or vacuum the rugs.

5. Dust or sweep the surfaces.

6. Wipe off the front door and the door handle.

7. Make note of how space might be better used by the addition of hooks, furniture, or baskets.

8. How could the entry space be more inspiring? Could you use a new lamp or entry table? Do you have items in your house that could be repurposed? Perhaps it needs new paint on the wall or door? A new rug? Put those items on your to-do list or want list for the future.

Get Organized Tips

Besides paper, what are the typical things you have in your hand when you walk in the door? Find solutions for each one.

- Set out a small tray for common things that get left on the table or lost in the house: keys, cell phone, wallet, sunglasses, a bus pass.
- Corral dog leashes and shoes in baskets.
- Place tote bags on hooks for things that need to be returned or donated.
- Designate spaces for backpacks, musical instruments, briefcases, purses, gloves, scarves, etc.

CELEBRATE! Treat yourself to something cheerful for your entry. Perhaps a new rug, a mirror for the wall, a small framed piece of art, a pot of seasonal plants or flowers on the porch, or a wreath on your door. Or paint your door a cheery teal blue or yellow. You'll feel welcomed and invited cheerfully into your home!

Make Room for Playing and Creating

FOCUS:
Creative Spaces

+ Hobbies
   and Crafts

+ Play Areas

The places where we play and create are often the most in need of paring down, decluttering, and organizing. When we have too much stuff in these spaces, it lessens the usefulness of the room and even stifles the creativity we dream about.

We need to make room do the things we want to do, right? If we aren't going to do "the things" or don't have room for them, it's time to part ways with all the things we hold on to just in case we ever want to do the things. Nobody has time to be overwhelmed by things that are not enhancing our life right now.

Create breathing room for what you love. You can tailor this mission to your own unique space with the type of clutter you have to deal with. You might be a crafter; you might not be. You might have kids; you might not. But whether you have a huge craft room or a small drawer for your tape and scissors, you'll want to create a dedicated and organized space for what will inspire your creativity.

Declutter and Organize Craft and Hobby Supplies

Here are eight easy steps to declutter and organize your craft and hobby supplies:

1. Spend as much time decluttering as you need to. I know we all like to get right to the more fun organizing part, but it will be much easier and more effective to know what to do next if you are fully decluttered first. If you have a lot

of supplies and hobby clutter, pick just one hobby or craft category at a time to declutter and reorganize.

2. Be honest about what crafts you have done recently. (Someday is not a day of the week. If you always think you'll use that needlepoint kit someday but you never really do, give it away to someone who will get good use out of it now.)

3. As you declutter, group items to keep by category (for crafting supplies you might have scrapbook paper, glue, glitter, gift wrap, ribbons, yarn, fabric, markers, tape, scissors, etc.).

4. If there is a craft or hobby you love, but you only have part of the supplies for it, take note of what is missing so you can have what you need when inspiration strikes.

5. Test out all supplies to make sure they all work (such as markers, glues, pens). Sharpen colored pencils. Throw out anything too old, broken, or ripped.

6. Less is more. You may not need as many duplicate supplies on hand as you have available right now. What could you part with?

7. Bring what you no longer need to a donation center or charity.

8. Designate an easily accessible spot for each craft and hobby.

Get Organized Tips

- If you don't have a designated room for crafts, a small basket, under-the-bed boxes, or even a secretary desk can provide space for your favorite craft or hobby.
- Shallow drawers for crafts make it easier to keep things organized, especially small items that can get easily lost.

- Pegboards, wall shelves, and hanging shoe organizers can maximize your vertical craft space.

- Use labels wherever helpful to organize crafts. If you want to invest in a label maker, it might come in handy throughout your house!

Set Up Areas for Play

Whether you have big or little kids, play is a part of childhood. Play is how children discover the world around them and helps them to learn more about themselves and the role they play. Your kids might need you to set up the time, space, and opportunity to play and learn. If you don't have kids, you can be the kid! What activities do you long for that you never seem to have time for?

1. How could you facilitate and encourage more creative play in the spaces you have? Do you have a space that needs to be decluttered and cleared out to make more room for play?

2. Make a list of the types of activities you would like your kids to be able to enjoy at home. Focus on having less random stuff, and provide more intentional opportunities to create and learn new skills through activities (such as building things, dress-up, role-playing, reading, drawing, painting, playing music or board games, cooking, doing outside exploration, etc.) to help kids (big and small) to explore and develop their own talent.

3. Decide which toys and activities your kids can have available to them to play with at will and which ones you'd like to bring out on a rainy day. Kids need free time to explore and opportunities to learn to make decisions about what they want to do, but you don't have to leave

everything out at all times. Just like us, kids can become overwhelmed by too many options.

4. Declutter games and toys that are not currently used or enjoyed. Simplify what you keep and use the opportunity to teach kids the importance of giving to others. It might help to move some items to another location for a short period of time to help ease the transition.

5. Keep organizational expectations age-appropriate and manageable to make it easy for your child to clean up their own toys. Too many labels, color-coding, organizational charts, or complicated systems may cause more frustration than they are worth.

Get Organized Tip

Over-the-door organizers and clear plastic bins are great for sorting your kids' favorite smaller toys, games, or activities.

Power Clean

Today's the day to give your craft, hobby, and play spaces a good cleaning! Whether it's just a desk to dust or an entire toy room to clean, get a rag and polish up the shelves and surfaces. Clean the windows, wash the curtains, vacuum the furniture and rugs, or sweep the floor.

CELEBRATE! Set aside designated time every day for your kids (or yourself) to focus on uninterrupted and unhurried play and creativity. Turn off the TV and other distractions, and help them to explore their creative options. Best of all, get in there and play with them!

Make Room for Feasting and Gathering

+ Organize by Zones

+ Declutter Cabinets

+ Organize Pantry

The kitchen and gathering spaces of our home are where we spend so much time making messes! Whether we are preparing meals, cleaning up, or gathering together as a family, these spaces deserve special attention to ambience. If they are disorganized, dirty, or cluttered, we won't be inspired to use them, let alone enjoy being in them.

How could you make more room for taking care of your family and inviting guests in? Take charge of the way your kitchen and gathering spaces are organized with these steps.

Reorganize Your Kitchen by Task Zones

Your kitchen is a hardworking space! No matter what size kitchen you have, it's helpful to organize your kitchen by the tasks you need to perform in it. When unrelated things are mixed together in every cupboard or drawer, you won't be very efficient.

Brainstorm what zones your kitchen might need and how they could be reimagined:

- a baking zone
- a cooking zone
- a food storage zone
- everyday dishes zone
- a coffee or tea zone

If your kitchen doesn't offer the space you need for every zone, set up creative organization destinations nearby or in an adjoining space, such as a freestanding cabinet or dining room. Start with paring down what you have so you'll have a better idea as to what you actually need.

Declutter and Organize Each Zone

Now that you know how you plan to designate space for each zone, it's time to declutter down to what will fit in each space. We'll focus on the pantry on another day, so break down your other zones—baking or cooking or dishes—and focus on decluttering them one at a time. Keep in mind where you'll be storing these items to make sure you pare down enough or have alternate storage available elsewhere.

Here are some creative ideas to maximize space. You can find cabinet organizers at IKEA, Target, dollar stores, and other home stores.

1. Save cupboard space by adding a hanging pot rack or hooks on the walls for frequently used pots.

2. Use easily stackable nesting bowls and measuring cups to best utilize drawer or cupboard areas. Items that don't nest take up excess space.

3. Hang open shelves in the kitchen or pantry to make the most of your kitchen's available vertical spaces.

4. Add a rolling freestanding island or kitchen cart with a drop leaf surface to expand counter space. Attach hooks or a towel rod to the side for additional storage.

5. Utilize the backs of cupboards by adding over-the-cupboard organizers, painting them with chalkboard paint for grocery lists, or posting a corkboard to pin recipes. Attach magnetic boards and magnetized spice holders to cabinet doors.

6. Add a wall-mounted magnetic knife holder to free up drawer or counter space.

7. Organize the area below the sink with rolling storage

drawers, risers, an over-the-cabinet basket, or a lazy Susan for cleaning supplies.

8. Place a crock by the stove to hold your most-used kitchen utensils to free up drawer space.

9. Add baskets in the empty spaces above your cabinets to keep items you use less often, such as turkey pans and holiday-themed cookie cutters.

10. Add a tension rod under the sink to hang cleaning bottles.

11. Add a hanging wall file organizer with slots to the inside of your cabinet to hold pan lids.

12. Add a lazy Susan for canned goods or spices.

13. Put risers inside kitchen cabinets as needed to optimize space. (IKEA sells shallow risers that work great for small cabinets and even refrigerators.)

Tidy Your Pantry

Whether you use a kitchen cabinet, a freestanding cupboard, or an entire walk-in pantry, how you organize your food matters to how efficient and organized you feel in your kitchen.

1. Toss out any old or expired spices or any food item that is unidentified or unknown.

2. Wipe off shelves.

3. Add glass jars, baskets, and containers for bulk food. Glass jars are attractive enough to sit on a counter or open shelf to save cabinet space.

4. Get a spice rack, or designate a drawer or a back-of-the-cupboard organizer. If you are short on space, pare down to a few essentials.

5. Organize food by categories: bulk items, spices, breakfast foods, baking, canned goods, snacks, soups. If you keep a

large pantry and it seems too overwhelming to do in one day, select one category to focus on at a time.

6. Label your glass jars and baskets with hanging tags or stickers (you can order tags or labels online).

7. Add over-the-door wire racks to doors for cans and extra pantry items.

8. To make it easy for the family to find their own breakfast, snacks, and lunch options in the pantry, group each of their choices together on a shelf, or put small items in a wire basket. This will ensure nothing gets hidden or lost in the back of a dark cabinet and makes it easy for everyone to find a quick snack for their lunch box.

9. Put a small plastic basket in the fridge for organizing cold lunch items, snacks, drinks, veggies, and fruit to take to school or work.

Get Organized Tips

Organize your dining and entertaining cabinets. Go through your dishes, serving pieces, glassware, flatware, linens, and pitchers and think about what you really love, what you really have room for, and what you really need. Consider paring down to one set of versatile dishes and switching up your look through the season with different cloth napkins, interesting salad plates, and other table decor.

Power Clean

1. Unload the dishwasher and put away all clean dishes. Load the dishwasher with all dirty dishes until you have an empty sink. Clean all pots and pans and wash anything that needs to be hand-washed.

2. Clean the stovetop.

3. Wipe down appliances and cabinets to clear fingerprints or smudges.

4. Wipe off all counters with your cleaning spray of choice.

5. Sweep floors and then mop or spray to shine them up.

6. Deep clean your sink. (For my white, cast-iron sink, I use Bon Ami cleaner to get scuff marks out. Check with your sink manufacturer for how to safely clean yours.)

7. Polish the faucet.

Reclaim Your Gathering Spaces

What is preventing you from enjoying gathering friends and family in your home? Let's tackle family living spaces and make them inspiring places to be!

1. Start with a clean sweep of all the surfaces to remove clutter, papers, dishes, unnecessary accessories, toys, or other pile-ups.

2. Look around and see how much more inviting your space is with clear surfaces!

3. Do you have excess or unused furniture in this room that might be contributing to an overly crowded or cluttered ambience? When a room has too many unnecessary pieces of furniture, there isn't breathing room to relax or enjoy gathering in that space. What could be relocated or rearranged to streamline and update this room? Give some

focused time to making more room to better utilize this space.

4. Consider what improvements you've been putting off or neglecting. It is hard to fully relax in or enjoy your room when you are overwhelmed by half-finished projects. An updated room will inspire you to keep it clean and organized, so beautifying your space is a win-win. What simple fixes and improvements could you cross off your to-do list?

Make a list of **SMART** goals to help you finish your projects and improve your gathering spaces. Rather than feeling overwhelmed by your to-do list or discontent because you have so much to do to finish this room, your **SMART** goals can help you pare down and improve your space one step at a time, with a realistic timetable and budget.

CELEBRATE! Once your room is organized and spic-and-span, celebrate by enjoying a quiet afternoon doing something you love. Or show off that beautifully tidy space by inviting your neighbors over for dinner!

Make Room Challenge Conclusion

Now that you've made it through the Make Room Challenge, I trust you are starting to find more room for what you really love at home, and in life, every day! High fives, friend! Will you let me know how you are doing? Use the hashtag #themakeroomchallenge to share on social media. Go to homelovestories.com to share and connect with me and other readers, and visit me at theinspiredroom.net. I can't wait to meet you there.

CELEBRATE! Give yourself a reward for your discipline and hard work. Perhaps a coffee date with a friend, or even something for your home, such as a new organizer for the bathroom, a set of replacement hangers or towels, or even do something creative, such as paint the inside of your closet an inspiring color or line some drawers with pretty paper, just for fun.

Find downloads and additional links to resources at
makeroomforwhatyoulove.com

Acknowledgments

I'm fortunate to be surrounded by a wonderful and supportive community.

I'm deeply grateful to my entire family, especially my husband, Jerry, and our amazing kids (Kylee, Courtney, Lance, and Luke), for making room for this grand adventure in our life! There are not enough words to describe how much I love you all. Extra thanks to Courtney from the bottom of my heart for everything you do for *The Inspired Room* and the gracious way you do it.

Thank you...

To my wonderful agent, Ruth Samsel, for representing me well. I appreciate your friendship, insights, and cheerleading along the way.

To the amazing publishing team at Harvest House. Your vision and heart for our partnership is a real blessing in my life. I'm grateful that you make room for me.

To Kim Moore, my editor. Your enthusiasm and encouragement along the way has been nothing short of inspiring.

To our project manager, Heather Green, for juggling these book projects with grace.

To Nicole Dougherty for your adorable hand-drawn art. Your talent for creating has made each project so special and fun!

To my sisters at (in)courage—so much love for you all (and for you too, Saul!).

To my blog community of writers and readers. I am so very thankful for your enthusiastic support and kindness. You make each blog post and every project a joy to create and share.

And, most of all, I'm grateful to my Savior. Thank you for your grace as I endeavor to make room in life for what matters most.

About the Author

Melissa Michaels is the creator and author of the popular home decorating blog *The Inspired Room*, which inspires women to love the home they have. Since 2007 Melissa has been encouraging hundreds of thousands of readers a month with daily posts and inspiration for all things house and home. *The Inspired Room* was twice voted as the *Better Homes and Gardens* magazine Reader's Choice decorating blog.

Melissa lives in Seattle with her husband, Jerry; their son, Luke; and two impossibly adorable Doodle pups, Jack and Lily, whose adventures are well loved and followed on their Facebook page (Facebook.com/jack.goldendoodle). The Michaels' daughters, Courtney and Kylee (and Kylee's husband, Lance), are an active part of *The Inspired Room*.

The Michaels family planted a church called Voyage in Bremerton, Washington, in 2009. They have created a unique and homey coffee shop environment for Voyage and are passionate about reaching out to emerging generations.

You can connect with Melissa and other home lovers through *The Inspired Room* (theinspiredroom.net) and use the subscribe option if you would like to have new, free blog posts delivered to your email inbox. You can also reach Melissa at melissa@theinspiredroom.com. Follow her at Facebook.com/theinspiredroom.fans and on Instagram, Pinterest, and Twitter as **theinspiredroom**.

A home isn't a showplace—it's a sanctuary.

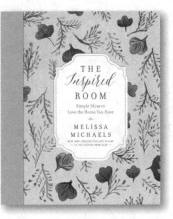

You're invited to forget about the rules and discover inspired ways to personalize your spaces and express your style with texture, color, and your favorite treasures. Room by room, you'll shape a home that is inspired by the people, beauty, and life you love.

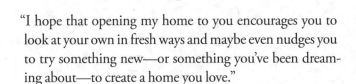

"I hope that opening my home to you encourages you to look at your own in fresh ways and maybe even nudges you to try something new—or something you've been dreaming about—to create a home you love."

Melissa

Create the Home of Your Dreams
Right Where You Are

You can love your home. Yes, the one with flaws, everyday messes, and maybe even a mix of hand-me-down furniture. Sure, it has some short-comings, but it also has a lot going for it—it's where your life, relation-ships, and dreams are being shaped.

Join Melissa Michaels, creator of the popular blog *The Inspired Room*, as she shares humor, lessons learned, and encouraging advice so you can:

- get motivated with the 31-day Love Your Home Challenge
- declutter, organize, and decorate your rooms with ease
- leap from dreamer to doer with confidence

Dare to see your surroundings with new eyes—it just might inspire a change of heart! Get ready to fall in love with the home you have.